DEVOTIONAL
PRAYERS

DEVOTIONAL

PRAYERS

WITH SCRIPTURE MEMORY VERSES

HENRY
THORNTON

EDITED AND INTRODUCED BY JAMES S. BELL, JR.

MOODY PRESS

CHICAGO

To my parents,
Jim and Kathryn,
who first taught me to pray

INTRODUCTION

s Christians, we know that we can freely share our needs, fears, and joys with a God who truly listens. We also know from His Word, the Bible, that He answers us in His own way. As a spiritual discipline, prayer is on the level of importance of studying God's Word, and we are reminded to pray without ceasing.

Yet if you are like me, you may feel vastly inadequate for the task; personal prayer may seem "dry" and unable to accomplish all the purposes it should. We get distracted and may come away feeling empty, thinking that prayer has become a duty rather than a joy. How can we "pray as we ought" and experience at least something similar to the praying saints of the past—people like Martin Luther, E.M. Bounds, or Madam Guyon?

Several years ago my wife found an old volume at a garage sale that has since become a great spiritual treasure to me. *Family Prayers and Prayers on the Ten Commandments* contains the actual morning and evening

7

prayers of Henry Thornton, a man in the class of saints listed above.

At first I felt that I couldn't have someone do my praying for me. Only later did I realize two truths to commend the reading and meditating on such prayers: much of the prayers contained the words inspired by the Holy Spirit (paraphrased Scripture), and the original *Family Prayers* superbly fulfilled the requirements of prayer: adoration, supplication, intercession, and thanksgiving.

After reciting these prayers each morning and evening, I found myself able to pray better spontaneously, often elaborating on the contents of the day's prayer. I have been able to meditate on the richness of these truths throughout the busy day.

The prayers exalt God for who He is and for the work of His Son. At the same time, the prayers help us to confess our needs for forgiveness, diligence, humility, charity, and many other needs. We are able to pray for the spread of the gospel, for our children, relations, government, and the suffering as well. The morning prayers help us focus on the importance of our daily calling in the light of eternity. Evening brings thanksgiving and self-examination, as well as the desire for peaceful rest in Christ. The cyclical pattern creates for me a rhythm so that I can encounter the Lord regularly, to both start and finish the day with Him.

Henry Thornton, though no longer remembered today, was a spiritual giant of his time when this book of prayers received wide circulation. Thornton was a central figure among a group of eminent and wealthy Anglican evangelicals of the nineteenth century known as the Clapham Sect. This group, which included William Wilberforce, met at Henry Thornton's home at Battersea

Rise in Clapham. They all acted upon the idea of "calling"—living out their faith in whatever occupation God placed them. Thornton was a prosperous banker and member of the British Parliament who composed these prayers for family devotions. One can only marvel at the depth of his spirituality and the training and impact he created upon the next generation.

Though you, the reader, can pray alone, family devotions are also appropriate, especially if the prayer segment of your gathering seems to lag. In modernizing the text, I have tried to retain the reverent and hallowed tone that is conducive to worship. I have also added his prayers on the Ten Commandments for devotional purposes. Though they will not earn heaven for us, God's law, says Jesus, is eternal. The Ten Commandments are His will for our lives and part of the sanctification process; thus we pray for His grace to know and keep them.

Thornton mentions the "Our Father" prayer and a doxology, and I have included them at the conclusion of the morning and evening prayers, respectively, to encourage you further to pray according to the Scriptures.

Finally, I have added a Scripture memory verse taken from the day's morning prayer to encourage meditation throughout the day. You may want to commit this verse to memory; consider putting it on a 3x5 card for convenient review throughout the day. In future months, as you reread the daily prayers, you can review the verses.

I pray that *Devotional Prayers* will bring a rich blessing to your devotional life.

JAMES S. BELL, JR.

Daily Prayers

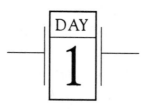

MORNING PRAYER

 LORD, God Almighty, the creator and ruler of the world, who has abundantly provided for the various wants of Your creatures, who has ordered the day and the night to succeed each other, and when You have refreshed man with sleep, requires him to pursue his work until the evening, we thank You that, while You have placed our lot in this life, You have not left us without hope in the world that is to come. We adore You for the gift of Jesus Christ Your Son, by whose gospel life and immortality are brought to light. We bless You for the pardon of sin through faith in a redeemer, for the guidance of Your providence, and for the consolations of your Spirit. We thank You for corporate worship, for Your written Word, and for all the other means of grace, which You have entrusted to us.

Grant that we may this day pursue, with faithfulness and diligence, that work which You have assigned to us;

and that we may, at the same time be spiritually and heavenly minded. In the midst of life we are in death. Let us remember this awful truth; and let us live this day as we shall wish that we had done, if it should, indeed, prove to be our last. Save us from the sins to which we are most prone. Do not leave us to the natural bent of our own minds, which are ever inclining us to evil; but put Your Spirit within us, and teach us to cultivate every Christian temper, and to abound in every good work.

Strengthen our faith in the glorious promises of the gospel, and fill us with that joy and peace in believing, which shall be more than a compensation for all the temporal sacrifices to which we may be called. Help us to bear affliction with a patient and quiet mind; or, if You should continue to give us prosperity, to be ever watchful over ourselves, and moderate in our enjoyments. And let us impart freely to others the good gifts that You shower down upon us.

Inspire us with zeal in the fulfillment of our relative duties, with integrity in our dealings, and the spirit of kindness to all men. Let us continually examine ourselves, and, advancing in self-knowledge, let us prevail over our infirmities and trials. Let us grow in grace, and in all goodness, and in meekness for Your heavenly kingdom.

We pray for Your blessing on all our friends and relations. May they also be filled with the knowledge of Your will, in all wisdom and spiritual understanding; and may we, and they, be of one heart, and one mind, loving each other as brethren in Christ, and uniting our efforts to promote both the good of all men and Your glory.

Have mercy on the poor and the afflicted, strengthen the weak, help the tempted, and guide the ignorant into the way of knowledge.

Bless the rising generation; save them from the dangers of this evil world and sanctify to them the events that they shall encounter. May they become instruments in Your hand for the advancement of the interests of Your church on earth, and members of Your blessed family in heaven.

We offer these humble and imperfect prayers in the name of Jesus Christ, our Lord and Savior. Amen.

OUR FATHER in heaven, hallowed be Your name. Your kingdom come. Your will be done on earth as it is in heaven. Give us this day our daily bread. And forgive us our debts, as we forgive our debtors. And do not lead us into temptation, but deliver us from the evil one. For Yours is the kingdom, and the power, and the glory, forever. Amen.

MEMORY VERSE

"The appearing of our Savior Jesus Christ, who has abolished death and brought life and immortality to light through the gospel" (2 Timothy 1:10).

EVENING PRAYER

LORD GOD, our heavenly Father, who are the maker of all things and the Judge of all men, we Your creatures, who live upon Your daily bounty and are accountable to You for all we do, desire now to offer up our acknowledgments of Your goodness during the past day, and to implore Your forgiving mercy.

We would be sorry for the trespasses that we have committed this day. You see, O Lord, all our hearts. We are blind and ignorant, prone to error, yet impatient of reproof. We often deceive ourselves with the mere appearance of goodness; but You know every false way in which we allow ourselves to walk. Pardon, we ask You, for Jesus Christ's sake, whatever evil we have either said, or thought, or done on this day. Pardon all the great number of our iniquities. Teach us continually to examine our lives by the light of Your unerring Word, and give unto us true repentance and faith in Jesus Christ.

We ask You, also, to fill us anew with Your Holy Spirit, that we may change our ways, and walk in the newness of life. You have favored us with much religious knowledge, and with many means of grace. O let us remember that unto whom much is given, of them shall much be required. Let us not live as the children of this world, employing our time in worthless and unprofitable things; but let us try to be useful in that station in which You have placed us. As we have received Christ Jesus the Lord, so let us walk in Him.

May we excel especially in those virtues, and abound in those works that His gospel has required. May we be full of meekness and patience, of kindness and forbearance, of benevolence and charity. Being established in the love of God, may we also love our neighbor with a pure heart, fervently. Let us not possess only that faith which is without works, and can profit neither ourselves nor those around us; but let us abound in all the fruits of righteousness, which are by Jesus Christ to the praise and glory of God.

We also beseech You to bless to us our activities, and so to order all things during our daily affairs, that they may result in our eternal good. We know not what a day may bring forth. Sanctify to us our prosperity and our adversity, our sickness and our health; whatever may be our trials, may we consider them as coming from Your fatherly hand, and never complain under them. May we maintain a cheerful and contented mind; and being reconciled to You our God, may we enjoy peace within ourselves, and be in right relationships with all people.

These our imperfect supplications we humbly present in the name of Jesus Christ our Savior. Amen.

*T*HE *grace of the Lord Jesus Christ, and the love of God, and the communion of the Holy Spirit be with you all. Amen.*

DAY 2

MORNING PRAYER

LMIGHTY AND ETERNAL GOD, our creator and preserver, and continual benefactor, we desire to begin this day with the acknowledgment of Your power and goodness, and of our obligation to love and serve You. We beseech You to grant us grace to pass the day in Your fear and in the fulfillment of Your commandments.

You have given to each of us our work in life; Lord, enable us diligently to perform our respective duties. Let us not waste our time in unprofitableness or idleness, nor be unfaithful to any trust committed to us. Let us not put on the mere appearance of goodness, nor try in any way to deceive those around us. But let us remember that Your eye is upon us, and let us have the testimony of our consciences, that in simplicity and godly sincerity we have our conversation in the world. Let truth be ever on our lips. Let us be examples of all integrity and uprightness. Help us, also, to perform a kind and Christian part towards those who may come under our influence. May we labor to do them service; and may we continually deny ourselves, that we may more effectively and abundantly minister to the various wants of others. May we rejoice with those who rejoice, and weep with those who weep, and be kindly affectionate to one another, with brotherly love, in honor preferring one another.

We also beseech You to give us patience to bear the several trials and tribulations of life, with a sound and contented mind. Let us not be perplexed with the cares of this world; nor overwhelmed with unnecessary fears; but let us ever trust Your gracious providence, and hope in Your goodness and mercy.

Give to us, when we are in prosperity, a spirit of moderation and generosity. Save us from pride, and from self-indulgence. Deliver us from the too great love of earthly things; and teach us to remember, that it is You who gives us all things richly to enjoy.

Bless the difficult circumstances through which we may pass. May we see Your hand in all Your various dispensations and adore You for the various events of Your providence, knowing that, if we truly love and serve You, all things shall work together for our good.

We submit to Your kind and fatherly care all our friends and relations. Direct their steps in life, and bless them with all spiritual blessings in Jesus Christ. Give to them the pardon of their sins and the blessed hope of eternal life.

We pray for the rising generation. May they remember their creator in the days of their youth; may they find You to be their refuge in all the events through which they pass.

Have mercy on all who are in any sorrow or trouble. We ask You to provide for them through the riches of Your mercy, and send special help in their hour of need.

Be favorable to this nation. Bless the president of the United States, and all who are in authority. Direct his advisers. Give wisdom to our Congress. Inspire our courts with integrity and our clergy with the spirit of true religion. Deliver us from the hands of all our enemies; and give us peace among ourselves.

We offer up our imperfect prayers in the name of Jesus Christ our Savior. Amen.

OUR FATHER in heaven, hallowed be Your name. Your kingdom come. Your will be done on earth as it is in heaven. Give us this day our daily bread. And forgive us our debts, as we forgive our debtors. And do not lead us into temptation, but deliver us from the evil one. For Yours is the kingdom, and the power, and the glory, forever. Amen.

MEMORY VERSE

"Rejoice with those who rejoice, and weep with those who weep" (Romans 12:15).

EVENING PRAYER

LORD, God Almighty, who knows all things, and understands the secrets of every heart, fit Your mercies, we pray, to our necessities; and grant unto all the members of this family such things as You see to be most needful for us.

We ask You especially to bring our hearts into full obedience to Your gospel. Take away from us all pride, hardness of heart, and unbelief; all undue love of this present world, all inordinate affection, and every evil inclination. Take from us every thing that is in opposition to the Spirit of Your grace.

May we humble ourselves as children in Your sight, receiving, in sincerity and simplicity of heart, the various doctrines of Your Word. Give us, also, grace to maintain a Christian spirit, and to abound in every good work. May we be patient and contented, thankful for our lot in life, praising and blessing You for all our providential as well as spiritual mercies. Continue Your favor upon us lest, by any evil habits which we indulge, we draw down Your anger upon us. Make us strict in our integrity, sincere in every word, faithful in every task, diligent in every duty, and amiable in every temper of our lives. May we be zealous to do honor to the cause of Your gospel; and thus to make the religion of Christ attractive.

Teach us to exercise all those virtues that shone so brightly in our Lord. At the same time, may we remember our exceeding sinfulness; and thus learn to bear with all the various infirmities of others. Give us grace, also, to declare, on proper occasions, our abhorrence of evil; and give us courage and integrity to exhort one another daily, unless any of us be hardened through the deceitfulness of sin. Teach us, in the spirit of love, to serve and edify one another.

And now, O Lord, wherever on this day we have failed in the performance of our duty, and in the exercise of any Christian temper, or wherever we have in any way offended You, we implore Your pardon, in the name of Jesus Christ.

Take us under Your protection this night; may we be safe under the shadow of Your wings; may we commit ourselves to You, in peace and comfort. May the gospel be our consolation, in our lying down, and in our rising up. May it be an ever-present source of happiness to us; may it lighten every trial, and reconcile us to every disappointment. May there be no place or time, no situation or circumstance, when the satisfaction that it imparts shall entirely leave us; but, being under its blessed influence, may our hearts be ever filled with thankfulness; and our lips with praises.

We ask every blessing, in the name of Jesus Christ our only Savior and our mediator. Amen.

THE grace of the Lord Jesus Christ, and the love of God, and the communion of the Holy Spirit be with you all. Amen.

DAY 3

MORNING PRAYER

O LORD, our heavenly Father, most gracious and merciful God, who has preserved us through all the stages of our past lives, and has blessed us with unnumbered benefits, being never weary of doing us good, give us grace to humbly and heartily thank You for all Your lovingkindness shown to us, and let us renew the solemn dedication of ourselves unto You.

We confess, before You, the sins of our lives, which are more than we can number or express. We lament the evil that, day by day, in thought, word, and deed we have committed against You. And we adore the riches of Your mercy, which forgives all our sins, heals all our iniquities, and still abounds even to us, who have so grievously rebelled against You.

We also pray that, while we rejoice in the thought of that exceeding goodness that is reveled in the gospel to us sinners, we may be in all respects transformed by the various doctrines of Your Word. Thus may we bring forth all those fruits of righteousness that bring, in Jesus Christ, praise and glory to Your name.

We pray that we may this day walk worthy of the Lord and that we may honor You by our patience under every trial, by our meekness under personal attack, and by our unwearied zeal in doing good. We pray that we may surrender our wills to Your most holy will in all things, readily accommodating ourselves to every new circumstance, which You, in Your providence, are pleased to send.

Grant that, through the daily contemplation of the doctrines of Your gospel, every good disposition may be formed in us. May the faith of Christ be effective to bring down our pride, to subdue our selfishness, to improve our temper, to direct and restrain our tongues, to motivate us with the purest zeal, and to fill us with charity toward our neighbor. May it also sanctify our daily work, providing the motive to do it, increasing our diligence in it, and teaching us to look to You, Lord, for our great and final reward. O God, bless us this day; and, not this day only, but to the end of our lives. Defend us in all our future dangers; help us in all our sorrows and adversities; lead us through every difficulty and trial.

If it pleases You to send us prosperity, enable us to devote the good things, which You give us, to Your service; and as You extend Your mercies, enlarge, also, the thankfulness of our hearts. Or, if it be Your righteous will either to try us with temptations or to give us strong afflictions, may we learn to bow meekly to Your gracious providence in all things. May we still trust Your unchanging purposes of mercy to us amidst all Your various dispensations.

To You, O God, who has been our support from our infancy, the help of our youth, and the guide of our advancing years, we commit ourselves to You for the days that are to come. Your providence has ordained our lot in life, and has ordered all things concerning us. Unto You, the same gracious God, we now resign all our affairs; to You we commend our bodies and souls, our temporal as well as our eternal interests. Especially, we ask You to save us from sin, as well as from those fears that our past transgressions might justly bring upon us.

We offer up these our prayers in the name of Jesus Christ, our Lord. Amen.

OUR FATHER in heaven, hallowed be Your name. Your kingdom come. Your will be done on earth as it is in heaven. Give us this day our daily bread. And forgive us our debts, as we forgive our debtors. And do not lead us into temptation, but deliver us from the evil one. For Yours is the kingdom, and the power, and the glory, forever. Amen.

MEMORY VERSE

"Now no chastening seems to be joyful for the present, but grievous; nevertheless, afterward it yields the peaceable fruit of righteousness to those who have been trained by it" (Hebrews 12:11).

EVENING PRAYER

REAT AND GLORIOUS GOD, we adore You for all Your infinite perfections. Righteous are You in all Your ways, and holy in all Your works! We are weak and helpless, sinful and guilty, exposed to danger on every side, and in continual need of Your gracious assistance.

Grant unto us a due sense of our dependence upon You; and enable us to lie down to rest, exercising faith in Your divine power, and in Your never-failing goodness. We desire to remember that Your eye sees us whereever we are; that You are around our bed, and are everywhere present with us. O Lord, pardon, for Jesus Christ's sake, the sins that You have seen in us this day. Many are the offenses that we continually commit, for we are, by nature, prone to evil; and our own hearts too often deceive us. But we desire to trust in the all-powerful mediation of Your blessed Son, who died for our sins and rose again for our justification, and who now lives at your right hand to make intercession for us. O Lord, grant to us peace with You, and a cheerful hope of being finally made partakers of everlasting life. May Your Holy Spirit give us comfort and dispose us to every good work.

Let us not return to sin, nor love the ways of ungodliness. Let us not allow ourselves any of those things that You have forbidden; instead, let us mortify all our corrupt affections, our pride and vanity, our anger and passion, our selfishness and worldliness. Let us put on, as the elect of God, mercy and lovingkindness, and tender compassion towards all men. Let us follow the example of our Savior's lowliness and meekness, of His holy zeal, His constant charity, His love to the souls of men. Let us daily improve, through Your grace, in every Christian grace; and let us practice in repentance for whatever we have done wrong.

Accept our thanks, O Lord, for the mercies of the past day, and for all Your goodness during our past lives. We bless You for every gift that You have bestowed upon us; for every deliverance that You have accomplished for any of us from pain and sickness, from sorrow and danger; and for every event that You have caused to work for our good. Be with us, we ask You, to the end of our days. Bless to us all the stages of life through which we pass. Make us humble in prosperity, and patient in adversity, grateful for all Your temporal mercies, but especially for Your unspeakable love in our redemption through Jesus Christ.

We commit to Your gracious care all our friends and relations. May we live in peace and harmony with them all—bearing each other's burdens, helping each other's infirmities, and ministering to each other's temporal and spiritual good.

Have compassion on the children of this family. Save them from the follies and dangers of youth, and make them obedient in all things. Prepare them for Your future service; and when they shall have done Your will on earth, may they be joint heirs with us in that inheritance which You have prepared for all who love You.

Hear us, O Lord, in these our prayers, for Jesus Christ's sake. Amen.

THE grace of the Lord Jesus Christ, and the love of God, and the communion of the Holy Spirit be with you all. Amen.

DAY 4

MORNING PRAYER

LMIGHTY LORD, our God, whose eyes are in every place seeing the evil and the good, and who sees not only our outward actions, but all our most secret thoughts, we ask You to maintain in us this day a constant sense of Your presence, and to preserve us from sinning against You. We are exposed to dangers by night and by day; our lives are in Your hands, and unto You we look for preservation from every evil. Lord, teach us to be ever mindful of You. When we go out and come in, and when we are alone and in company, may we bear in mind that You are continually with us and that You take account of all we think and speak and do.

We ask You, merciful Father, to pardon our past sins, for Jesus Christ's sake. When we reflect how strict and holy is Your law, and how often we have yielded to anger and passion, to pride and vanity, or to the desire of some forbidden thing, we are filled with shame and guilt

31

on account of our many trespasses against You. But we desire to bless Your holy name, that You have not left us without hope; for You have revealed Yourself to us, as pardoning iniquity, transgression, and sin, for the sake of Your Son, Jesus Christ. We therefore ask You now to receive us into Your favor, and to make us draw close to You through Jesus Christ.

We know that we draw near unto You by trusting in Christ's name, and not in our own righteousness. We ask You, for His sake, to strengthen our weakness, and to enable us this day to fulfill every duty to which we are called. May we be kind and affectionate one to another, sincere and upright in all our dealings, and diligent in our proper work. May we rejoice in every opportunity of doing good; and may we have grace to deny ourselves, that we may the more abundantly minister to the wants of others. Put into us a spirit of compassion for the poor, as well as of thankfulness to You, who has amply provided for us. Teach us to forgive those who have injured us, since we ourselves have so many sins for which we hope to be forgiven. Raise us up to be instruments in Your hand for the good of many. May we rejoice in the sense both of Your pardoning mercy and Your constant and special protection.

We ask You, Lord, to look down in compassion on all our dear friends and relations. Bestow upon them all things that You know to be needful for them. Sustain and comfort them in this life; but especially, give to them the blessings of the life to come.

Bless our president. Direct the public councils of the nation. Give success to every effort to relieve the oppressed, and to establish righteousness and peace on the earth.

Have mercy on the young. Grant that they may be trained in the nurture and admonition of the Lord and may thus learn to do Your will, and to walk in Your fear, all the days of their lives; and to hand down Your truth to the next generation.

O Lord, we beseech You to bring us all, by the great number of Your mercies, through this world of many temptations and trials, to that place of everlasting rest and peace, which You have prepared for them who love You.

We offer up these our humble supplications, in the name of and through the mediation of our Lord and Savior, Jesus Christ. Amen.

OUR FATHER in heaven, hallowed be Your name. Your kingdom come. Your will be done on earth as it is in heaven. Give us this day our daily bread. And forgive us our debts, as we forgive our debtors. And do not lead us into temptation, but deliver us from the evil one. For Yours is the kingdom, and the power, and the glory, forever. Amen.

MEMORY VERSE

"Draw near to God and He will draw near to you. Cleanse your hands, you sinners, and purify your hearts, you double-minded" (James 4:8).

EVENING PRAYER

LMIGHTY AND EVERLASTING GOD, You are unspeakably great and glorious. You are the king, eternal, immortal, and invisible. Your throne is in the highest heavens, and You are exalted above all blessing and praise. We, the creatures whom Your hand has made, and whom Your providence sustains from day to day, desire at this time humbly to bow down before Your divine majesty. We acknowledge our obligations to Your infinite goodness and mercy.

We bless You for all the comforts of this life but, above all, for Your overwhelming love in sending Your Son from heaven to become the Savior of our souls. We thank You for having provided this mediator, through whom sinners may draw near to You. We beseech You, O Lord, to grant unto us pardon of our sins through Jesus Christ. Forgive us the transgressions of this day and may Your Holy Spirit fill us anew, that we may be enabled to love You with all our hearts; and faithfully to perform Your righteous will.

We ask You to renew us in the spirit of our minds. Help us to put off the old man, which is corrupt according to the flesh, and to put on the new man, which is created after Your own image in righteousness and true holiness. Deliver us from blindness and hardness of heart, from too great a love of this present world, as well as from coldness and laziness in Your service. May Your blessed Spirit produce in us a deep and sincere repentance; and make us fruitful in every good word and work.

We also ask You to enable us to put our whole confidence in You. May we commit all our concerns into Your merciful hands, who are ever ready to protect those who sincerely love and serve You. Let Your watchful providence defend us by night and by day, in adversity and prosperity, in sickness and in health; and, whenever the sacred hour of our death shall draw near, may we find our consolations in Christ are many.

We most humbly address You, in behalf of all those for whom it is our duty to pray. We would intercede with You for our native land, that it may still be favored with the light of Your gospel. Let the seeds of divine knowledge sown in it bring forth abundant fruit. Bless the president of the United States, and all in authority; and give them wisdom to fulfill the arduous duties to which they are called. Have mercy on all who are in sorrow: on the widows and the fatherless, and on those who have none to help them. Look down with compassion on those who suffer from the calamities of war. Be merciful to our dear friends and relations. Let the light of Your gospel shine into all their hearts. Grant that they may be now united with us in the bonds of Christian love; and that we may all be members of Your blessed family in heaven.

We beseech You to take us under Your care this night. We are unable to protect ourselves; but You, Lord, are ever present with us. Hear us from heaven Your dwelling place; and, for Your mercy's sake, bestow upon us more than we are able to ask, or think, or are worthy to receive.

We present these our humble and imperfect prayers, in the name of our Lord and Savior, Jesus Christ. Amen.

THE grace of the Lord Jesus Christ, and the love of God, and the communion of the Holy Spirit be with you all. Amen.

DAY 5

MORNING PRAYER

LORD, God Almighty, enable us, we ask You, to call upon You with humble and devout hearts. Let us not mix any worldly or wandering thoughts with the supplications that we offer up to You, but let us remember that we are now in Your presence, and let us worship You in spirit and in truth.

We thank You, O God, for Your mercy to us during the past night. We bless You for our renewed health and strength, and for the various comforts that surround us. And we desire now to dedicate again to You all the faculties of our bodies and of our minds and to spend the day that is before us to Your glory.

Deliver us from all the temptations of the day. Help us to resist the world, the flesh, and the devil. Let us not be drawn aside to any thing that is contrary to our Christian duty, either by the tendency to sin that is within us, or by the evil example of those around us; but let us watch and strive continually, that all our ways may be pleasing in Your sight. We confess that we are weak and helpless and filled with iniquity. For our merciful Savior's sake, have compassion on our infirmities, and give us grace sufficient for us in every hour of our necessity. O Lord, grant that we may thus be preserved from sin and, putting our trust in Thee, may not be disappointed.

Give us faith in all the truths of Your Word; may we be daily warned by the terrors of the Lord, and encouraged by Your mercy. May we meditate on the awful punishments denounced against the wicked, and call to mind the reward that You have promised to those who please You by patient continuance in well-doing. And thus may we be prepared to make every sacrifice to which You may be pleased to call us. May we cut off our right hand and pluck out our right eye when You require us to do it. And may we consider all our interests in this life as of no value compared with the eternal welfare of our souls. May we seek first the kingdom of God and His righteousness, trusting that all things needful for the body shall be added unto us.

Pardon, O Lord, all our sins in time past; we pray for mercy, in the name of Jesus Christ; and we bless You for this great mediator, in whom we would place all our confidence and hope.

We ask every blessing in the name of the same Lord and Savior. Amen.

OUR FATHER in heaven, hallowed be Your name. Your kingdom come. Your will be done on earth as it is in heaven. Give us this day our daily bread. And forgive us our debts, as we forgive our debtors. And do not lead us into temptation, but deliver us from the evil one. For Yours is the kingdom, and the power, and the glory, forever. Amen.

MEMORY VERSE

"God is Spirit, and those who worship Him must worship Him in spirit and in truth" (John 4:24).

EVENING PRAYER

LMIGHTY AND EVERLASTING GOD, who are of purer eyes than to behold iniquity, yet has promised forgiveness to all those who repent of the evil that they have done, we draw near to You under a deep sense of our unworthiness. We have transgressed in thought, word, and deed; and when we look back on our past lives, we are confounded by the multitude of our offenses. Many have been the sins of which You and You only have been the witness. Lord, save us from that wrath that we have merited. You do not will the death of sinners, but rather that they should turn from wickedness and live. Fulfill towards each of us those gracious promises that You have made in Jesus Christ, and enable us to rejoice, in the sense of Your favor here, and in the hope of eternal life in the world to come.

And lest, through our frailty, we should again yield to the power of our many temptations, grant unto us both the guidance of Your providence and the help of Your Holy Spirit. Put into our hearts good desires; and enable us, by Your grace, to bring these desires to good use. Correct whatever is in us that dishonors You. Deliver us from pride and vanity, from the too great love of earthly things, from that fear of man, which brings a snare, and from all inordinate indulgence. Save us from envy, hatred, and malice. Let not the sun go down upon our wrath. Let us go to rest this night, full of charity and good will, and maintaining a conscience void of offense towards You and towards all men. May our hearts be a fit habitation for Your Spirit, and may our souls and bodies be preserved blameless unto the coming of our Lord Jesus Christ.

With these prayers for ourselves, we offer up our intercessions for others also. Let the light of Your gospel shine upon all mankind. Have mercy on this land. Bless our president and all in authority under him. Strengthen their hands, that they may effectively repress wickedness and vice, and maintain Your true religion among us. Give grace to all ministers of the gospel, that they may both preach Your Word and be examples of virtue and godliness. Send down Your blessing, both temporal and spiritual, upon our many relations and friends; and unite with us in Christian bonds those who are already joined to us by the ties of nature and affection. Be merciful to those who are in any trouble of mind, body, or estate.

Regard in tender compassion the young of this family. May they daily learn the fear of the Lord; and may they ever walk in Your commandments.

We now ask You to continue to give us Your gracious protection through this night. Into Your hand we commend our bodies, and our souls; our temporal, and our eternal interests. You, O Lord, neither slumber nor sleep; now take us all under Your special care, defend us from every danger, and grant us such refreshing sleep that we may be fitted for the duties of the following day. And give us grace so to live, that we may never be afraid to die; but that whether we live, we may live unto the Lord; or whether we die, we die unto the Lord. We ask for Your grace in the name, and through the mediation of Jesus Christ, our blessed Savior. Amen.

THE grace of the Lord Jesus Christ, and the love of God, and the communion of the Holy Spirit be with you all. Amen.

DAY 6

MORNING PRAYER

O LORD, God Almighty, infinite in power, in goodness, and in mercy, help us now to worship You with reverence and humility. Before You the angels veil their faces. May we, therefore, approach You with a deep sense of Your awesome majesty, and of Your spotless purity and holiness; and may we so address You that You may hear our prayers and pour down Your blessing upon us.

We ask You, O Lord, to grant us this day Your Holy Spirit, that we may be strengthened to fulfill our several duties, and to resist the temptations that may come upon us. We call upon You, in the name of Jesus Christ, through whom You give strength to the weak, and supply all the spiritual wants of the soul. Have compassion upon us, for our Savior's sake; and give us grace to do whatever You require of us. O cleanse us, for His sake, from the stain of every sin, from pride and envy, from malice, selfishness, and uncharitableness. Make us meek, lowly, gentle, kind, and forgiving. Let us not live to please ourselves, or indulge any evil inclinations of our own hearts; but let us aim to glorify You, our God, and to do good in our generation.

You have appointed, unto each of us, our work in life. We pray, that we may have grace to fulfill, each of us, the duties of our several stations, with integrity and fidelity. May we remember that this day Your eye is continually upon us; and, as we think of You, may we put our cheerful trust in You, and commit all our ways unto You, and be found in the fear of the Lord all the day long.

We desire to acknowledge Your various mercies to us. We bless You, that You cover our table with plenty, that You allow us to abound with the good things of this life, and cause us to go out and come in in safety. O Lord, help us to use, with moderation, the gifts that You bestow, and to maintain continual thankfulness of heart as we enjoy them.

Especially, we bless You for Your mercies in Jesus, by whom we obtain pardon of sin and the blessed hope of eternal life. We beseech You, for His sake, to give us a right understanding in all things, that we may know how to walk so as to please You and how to avoid all that is hateful in Your sight. Guide us in all difficulties; and strengthen us under all temptations; and supply You our spiritual, as well as temporal wants, for Your great mercy's sake in Jesus Christ our Lord. Amen.

OUR FATHER in heaven, hallowed be Your name. Your kingdom come. Your will be done on earth as it is in heaven. Give us this day our daily bread. And forgive us our debts, as we forgive our debtors. And do not lead us into temptation, but deliver us from the evil one. For Yours is the kingdom, and the power, and the glory, forever. Amen.

MEMORY VERSE

"Commit your way to the Lord, trust also in Him, and He shall bring it to pass" (Psalm 37:5).

EVENING PRAYER

LMIGHTY AND EVERLIVING GOD, author of our being, supporter of our lives, and source of all our hopes both in this world and in that which is to come, we lift up our evening prayer to You. We acknowledge Your divine goodness and our continual dependence upon You.

We thank You for Your merciful protection this day. By You have we been sustained ever since we were born, and by Your gracious care we are now enabled to lie down in peace. We are exposed to dangers on every side: to innumerable ills, which afflict the body, and to many sorrows of the mind. We live in the midst of an ensnaring world: our own hearts are ever ready to deceive us, and our great spiritual adversary goes about seeking whom he may devour. O Lord, our hope and confidence are only in You. Be to us a rock of defense, that we may be saved from the power of our enemies. In every period of temptation, in the period of adversity and in the time also of prosperity, in the hour of death, and in the day of judgment, good Lord, deliver us.

We ask You to pardon the sins that we have this day committed. Although we profess to love Your name, yet in many things we continue to offend You. We often hear Your holy Word and are instructed in every part of Your sacred truth. Yet we bring forth little fruit that is worthy of our Christian calling and of that care which You in Your grace have bestowed upon us. We earnestly implore Your pardon, in the name of Jesus Christ. Be merciful to us, and send Your Holy Spirit into our hearts, that we may more deeply repent, and may reform our lives, and be disciples of Christ not in name only, but in deed and in truth.

Be pleased to sanctify to the good of our souls the events of this day. May we be gathering wisdom from the scenes that we see around us. When we behold instances of patience and longsuffering, of meekness and gentleness, of lovingkindness and charity, may we follow them; and when we witness the mortality of others, may we be reminded that our time also is short, and that blessed is that person whom his Lord, when He comes, shall find watching.

We earnestly ask You, bless our several friends and relations. Be generous to our benefactors.

Show Your special mercy to the children of this family. Give wisdom to those who shall be appointed to instruct them; and provide for them friends who shall guide them in the right way, and shall prove a blessing to the end of their lives.

We pray for the president of the United States, that he may experience Your best blessings; for our Congress, that their counsels may be directed to our true interests, and to Your glory; for our magistrates, that they may not fail to be a terror to evildoers. We offer praise for them who do well: for the ministers of the gospel, that they may go forth in Your strength, and preach Your pure and unadulterated Word, and have abundant success; for our great men, that they may be examples of virtue to those beneath them; for the poor, that they may be preserved from complaining at their lot, and may live in all godliness and honesty; and for those who are sick or in trouble, that they may patiently endure the afflictions of the Lord, and in due time find deliverance. We thus commend to Your gracious care both ourselves and others; and we desire to lie down in perfect charity with all men.

O Lord, hear us in these our prayers, for Jesus Christ's sake, to whom, with You and the Holy Ghost, be all honor and glory, world without end. Amen.

THE grace of the Lord Jesus Christ, and the love of God, and the communion of the Holy Spirit be with you all. Amen.

MORNING PRAYER

LORD, God Almighty, who has safely brought us to the beginning of another day, we ask You to conduct us through this day in peace. Enable us, also, to pass all the time of our pilgrimage on earth in such a way that, when we pass from this world, we may be prepared to meet You in Your heavenly kingdom. When we think of this life and its various temptations, when we look around and see the wickedness of the world, and then contemplate also the weakness and corruption of our nature, we might well sink through fear of the difficulties with which we have to struggle, and tremble lest we should fall under the power of our many temptations. But we bless You, O Lord, for that abundant grace that is treasured up for us in Jesus Christ. We thank You for all the motives, promises, and encouragements afforded us in Your gospel, and we would daily rejoice in it as the power of God to salvation for everyone who believes. We bless You, that Your Son has died as a sacrifice for sin; and that the Spirit of Christ is sent to sanctify us. We, therefore, now pray for the filling of the Holy Spirit; that we may go forth to our daily occupations and trials, having the Lord for our righteousness and our strength.

Prepare us, we ask You, for every duty of this day; arm us for every trial which may come upon us. Sanctify us, O Lord, in body, soul, and spirit. May we now seriously devote ourselves to You; and may we be found walking in Your fear all the day long, fulfilling, each of us, our proper work with Christian humility and simplicity. Deliver us from a careless and unbelieving life; from a life of idleness and unprofitableness, as well as of wickedness and vice. Save us from the sins that in times past may have most easily beset us and from those temptations to which we may now, through our age and circumstances, be most exposed.

May our hearts be filled with love to You; and may all our abilities be so employed in doing good that no place may be given for those temptations that continually overcome those who do not know the gospel of salvation.

And may Your grace increase in us and our corruptions be weakened, day by day. At the same time, forgetting the things that are behind and looking forward to those things before us, may we continue to press toward the mark of the prize of our high calling in Christ Jesus.

We also beseech You to deliver us from every prejudice and error by which we may be in danger of being deceived. Save us from a blinded conscience and a false and misguided zeal. Suffer not that, through our fault, the way of truth should ever be evil spoken of; and make us fearful unless we hinder the gospel of Christ.

O Lord, help us also this day to remember how short and uncertain is the time of our journeying here on earth, so that, whatever our hands find to do, we may do it with all our might. May we fulfill zealously the duties of our stations in life, and, at the same time, may we maintain a spiritual and heavenly mind. May we often think of that blessed region where Christ sits at the right hand of God; and, whether we eat, or drink, or whatever we do, may we do all to Your glory. Amen.

We offer up these our humble and imperfect prayers in the name of Jesus Christ, our Lord.

OUR FATHER in heaven, hallowed be Your name. Your kingdom come. Your will be done on earth as it is in heaven. Give us this day our daily bread. And forgive us our debts, as we forgive our debtors. And do not lead us into temptation, but deliver us from the evil one. For Yours is the kingdom, and the power, and the glory, forever. Amen.

MEMORY VERSE

"For I am not ashamed of the gospel of Christ, for it is the power of God unto salvation for everyone that believes, for the Jew first and also for the Greek" (Romans 1:16).

EVENING PRAYER

LMIGHTY AND EVERLASTING GOD, who sees all our thoughts and words and works, and who will judge us at the last day, we ask You to pardon any sins we have this day committed against Your divine majesty and to give us grace to examine ourselves, that we may know where we have offended against You.

We fear that we have this day done many things which we ought not to have done, and have left undone many things which we ought to have done. We may have indulged our pride and our evil tempers; we may have harbored many sinful thoughts; we may have been negligent in the performance of the duties of our calling; and may have omitted opportunities for doing good. We profess to be Your servants, but how great a part of our duty do we often leave unperformed! O pardon our offenses, for Jesus Christ's sake; and teach us continually to correct our lives, that we may become His disciples, not in name only, but in deed and in truth.

We ask You to take us under Your gracious care this night; we are surrounded by dangers; and are at all times unable to help ourselves; but You are ever present with those who put their trust in You. How many are there who will pass this night in sorrow and in pain! How many who will mourn through the uncertainty of their hearts and are without any sure hope in their God. O Lord, grant to us, if it please You, refreshing rest; but especially teach us to put our trust in You.

Enable us to rejoice in our most merciful Savior, amidst all the trials that we may encounter here; and to look forward with humble and cheerful hope to the great day of our appearing before You. May we know in whom we have believed; and may our souls be safe in the hands of that redeemer to whom we have committed them; and in whose merits alone we desire to trust. Accept, also, for His sake, the imperfect services of this day; pardon what has been evil in us; and look down with favor on what has been good, since we present unto You even our best works only in the name of Jesus Christ, Your Son.

We ask You to have mercy on our dear friends and relations, to relieve their sorrows, and to supply their wants, as well as to direct their steps. Grant to them a lively faith in the promises of Your gospel, and make them fruitful in every good work.

We pray for our president and country. O Lord, deliver us from the hands of our enemies, and direct the public measures to our true interests and to Your glory.

Have pity on the poor, the desolate, and the oppressed. Be a father to the fatherless and a God of consolation to the widow. Look down with an eye of favor on the rising generation, and raise up a seed to serve You who shall hand down Your truth to the latest posterity.

Bless especially the children of this family. May they be trained up in the nurture and admonition of the Lord; may they be submissive and dutiful in all things; may they live in harmony and love, one towards another; may they be kept from the pollution of the world; and, after a life of holy obedience to Your laws, may they all be made members of Your blessed family above.

O Lord, pardon the infirmity of these our prayers and answer us, not according to what we either desire or deserve, but according to the riches of Your grace in Jesus Christ; for whom we bless You, and to whom, with You, and the Holy Ghost, be all honor and glory, world without end. Amen.

THE grace of the Lord Jesus Christ, and the love of God, and the communion of the Holy Spirit be with you all. Amen.

DAY 8

MORNING PRAYER

LORD, God Almighty, we ask You now to deliver us from all wandering thoughts. Help us to remember in whose presence we are; and let us worship You in spirit and in truth.

O Lord, our heavenly Father, who are the preserver of our lives and the giver of all the good things that we enjoy, we thank You for the mercies of the past night. We bless Your name, that we are meeting together in so much health and comfort and that we have now the prospect of passing another day in the enjoyment of the bounties of Your providence. We also set before us the blessed hope of everlasting life.

We ask You to give us this day grace to serve You in our several stations, and to walk according to the gospel of Jesus Christ. Save us from the temptations of the day; strengthen us for the fulfillment of our duties; direct us in all our difficulties; and comfort us under any trouble or adversity, into which we may this day come. Grant that when we lie down at night, we may be able to look back on the hours that shall have passed with a humble confidence that You accept our services and will pardon our infirmities, for Jesus Christ's sake.

We ask You to deliver us from all evil passions, from pride and envy, from hatred and ill will, from fault finding and uncharitableness, and especially from the want of Christian kindness towards those who dwell with us in the same family, and worship You as partakers of the same faith. Preserve us, also, from those secret transgressions that Your eye alone can discern in us. Deliver each of us from the sins that most easily beset us. O Lord, grant that Your good Spirit may this day abide within us, and dispose us to every good work.

And help us also to call often to remembrance the great love of our Lord and Savior, Jesus Christ, who came down from heaven to die for us, that we, being delivered from the dread of Your wrath, and rejoicing in the hope of Your mercy, might serve You day by day, in newness of life. O Lord, strengthen our faith in Him who has suffered on the cross for us. Teach us to walk according to His example. May we, like Him, be kind and compassionate, forbearing and forgiving, holy and blameless, undefiled and separate from sinners.

And bless us, not this day only, but to the end of our lives. We pray that so long as we remain in this world of trial You would strengthen us by Your Holy Spirit, and comfort us, and continually direct us. Help us not, at any time, to depart from You, who are our Father and our God, through any allurements of the world, or any temptations of the flesh, or of the devil. Rather make us ever steadfast in Your truth, and faithful to Your cause, and devoted to Your service.

We offer up these our imperfect prayers, in the name and through the mediation of our only Savior, Jesus Christ. Amen.

OUR FATHER in heaven, hallowed be Your name. Your kingdom come. Your will be done on earth as it is in heaven. Give us this day our daily bread. And forgive us our debts, as we forgive our debtors. And do not lead us into temptation, but deliver us from the evil one. For Yours is the kingdom, and the power, and the glory, forever. Amen.

MEMORY VERSE

"As His divine power has given to us all things that pertain to life and godliness, through the knowledge of Him who has called us to glory and virtue" (2 Peter 1:3).

EVENING PRAYER

LORD GOD ALMIGHTY, Father of mercies, from whom we derive the temporal comforts that we enjoy, and to whom we owe the blessed and glorious hope of everlasting life, we desire to render to You this our evening sacrifice of prayer, and praise, and thanksgiving. We acknowledge Your goodness to us during the past day; and we beseech You to continue to us Your gracious protection during the darkness and silence of the approaching night. You are ever present with us. You sustain our lives, though we do not see You. You are our protection in all dangers. You are our support in trouble, our guide in difficulty, our best consolation in time of sickness, and our only refuge in the hour of death.

We ask You to increase our trust and confidence in You. Deliver us from the love of this changing and uncertain world. Strengthen our faith in the great promises of Your gospel, and grant that, having committed ourselves to Your mercies in Jesus Christ, we may find in Him continual rest and peace.

We ask You, for His sake, to pardon whatever sins we have this day committed against You. Although we profess to know Your Word, and to live in obedience to your will, in many things we continue to offend. We are often slothful in the performance of our duties; we fail to guard against our particular temptations; we yield to the evil example of those around us; we gratify our pride; we indulge our evil tempers; we renew our sins, to the great unrest of our souls. O Lord, forgive, for Jesus Christ's sake, the offenses of this day; and pour out upon us Your Holy Spirit, that we may become more steadfast and zealous in Your service, and more diligent in every good work.

We commit to Your gracious and fatherly care all those for whom it is our duty to pray. Have compassion on our dearest relations and friends. Supply their various wants through the riches of Your mercy in Jesus Christ.

Bless our president, and all who are in authority; and give them wisdom to fulfill the arduous duties to which they are called.

Be merciful to all who are in sorrow. Look down with pity on those who suffer through the calamities of war, on prisoners and captives, and on all who are destitute and oppressed. Bestow Your special favor on Your afflicted servants, and cause their earthly troubles to bring about their eternal joy.

Have mercy on the young; may there be never wanting in this land a seed to serve You; and may those who shall come after us obtain from You an increase of light and knowledge, as well as of faith, and hope, and love. In this way may the fruits of righteousness abound, and may the excellency of Your gospel be made known more and more to the world.

We present unto You these our imperfect supplications, in the name of Jesus Christ, our Lord. Amen.

THE grace of the Lord Jesus Christ, and the love of God, and the communion of the Holy Spirit be with you all. Amen.

DAY 9

MORNING PRAYER

GOD, who has commanded us in Your Word to call upon Your name, and has declared that You hear and answer the prayers of those who make their supplications to You, we desire now to offer up our petitions, under a deep sense of our unworthiness, and of Your manifold and great mercies.

We bless You for Your preservation of us during the past night; and we desire to acknowledge again our dependence upon You, and our sincere obligations toward You. We thank You for having poured down upon us so many blessings of this life. We thank You for our health and strength, for our food and clothes, and for all the comforts and conveniences that we enjoy. But above all we praise You for the inestimable privilege of being born in a land of religious freedom. For these, and for all Your various and great mercies, we would render to You a grateful heart; and we would attempt to show our gratitude, not with our lips only, but with our lives, by giving up ourselves to Your service, and by walking before You, in holiness and righteousness, all our days on earth.

We now ask You to enable us by Your grace to pass the whole of this day in honor of You. May we employ ourselves in doing those things that fit our station and circumstances; may we mortify all our corrupt affections; may we diligently attempt to maintain a conscience void of offense toward You and toward all men; may we rise superior to our temptations; and, by Your grace, prevail over our many infirmities.

We ask You, O Lord, to stimulate our minds by those glorious hopes set before us in Your Word; so that if we have any present sacrifices to make, they may seem small to us in comparison with that inward satisfaction and joy that the gospel gives in the midst of worldly disappointments. And, at the same time, deliver us from every false hope. May we examine well our title to heaven, till we know that our foundation is sure, and shall never fail us. We confess that we are daily surrounded with infirmity; but we pray that every evil habit may be weakened in us, that every temptation may, by degrees, be overcome, and that every terror may finally be done away. May we thus be brought into the true liberty of the children of God and serve You without fear, in holiness and righteousness, all the days of our lives.

Hear, O Lord, these our prayers; and supply both our temporal and spiritual wants, for the sake of Jesus Christ, our blessed Savior. Amen.

OUR FATHER in heaven, hallowed be Your name. Your kingdom come. Your will be done on earth as it is in heaven. Give us this day our daily bread. And forgive us our debts, as we forgive our debtors. And do not lead us into temptation, but deliver us from the evil one. For Yours is the kingdom, and the power, and the glory, forever. Amen.

MEMORY VERSE

"I myself always strive to have a conscience without offense towards God and men" (Acts 24:16).

EVENING PRAYER

LMIGHTY AND EVERLASTING GOD, by whose power we were created, by whose providence we are sustained, and by whose grace in Christ we are made heirs of eternal life, we desire to bless You for all Your mercies, both temporal and spiritual, and especially for Your goodness to us on the day that is now past.

We thank You for our food and clothes, for our various comforts and enjoyments; for our freedom from pain and sorrow, and for our deliverance from many of those temptations that are common in the world. We bless You also for the religious advantages that we so abundantly enjoy, for the light that shines around us, for the various means of grace, and for the gift of Your written Word.

We desire, at the same time, to confess our numberless sins. We have trespassed in thought, word, and deed; we have done that which we ought not to have done; we have left undone that which we ought to have done; and our only hope is in Your mercy. Pardon, O Lord, for Christ's sake, all the evil that we have committed on this day. Forgive whatever pride and vanity we may have indulged; whatever anger and passion, whatever worry and impatience, we may have betrayed; and whatever evil thoughts we may have harbored in our minds. Pardon, also, the various sins of our words by which we so often violate the law of charity toward our neighbor. We plead the merits of Jesus Christ, Your Son; and we would rejoice that there is this great mediator between God and man, through whom there is perfect remission of sins for all those who, with penitent and contrite hearts, confess their trespasses against You.

And grant, we ask You, that we may attempt continually to amend our lives, and to walk in the way of Your commandments. Put within us Your Holy Spirit, that we may turn from every sin and may delight in doing the will of our heavenly Father. Make us humble and lowly, kind and generous, and fruitful in every good work. May we follow the example of our blessed Savior, who went about doing good; and remembering how short is the time of our journey here in earth, may we use all diligence both in serving others, and in making our own calling and election sure.

We desire also, before we lay down to rest, to commend to Your grace and your care all our dear friends and relations. We ask You to protect them from all evil;

and to grant to them all things needful for them; and, when they shall have experienced Your favor here, to bring them to Your everlasting kingdom.

Bless the children of this family: strengthen them, that they may resist sin, deny themselves, and bring forth fruit in their lives to the praise and glory of Your name.

And, finally, we implore Your blessing on our president and country, on our Congress, our courts, our ministers of the gospel, and all ranks of people among us. Teach us to carry out our tasks with fidelity; and to walk in the fear of God, and in charity toward all fellow creatures.

We offer up these our imperfect prayers and supplications, in the name of Jesus Christ, our Lord and Savior. Amen.

THE grace of the Lord Jesus Christ, and the love of God, and the communion of the Holy Spirit be with you all. Amen.

DAY 10

MORNING PRAYER

LMIGHTY AND EVERLASTING GOD, we kneel down to thank You for Your merciful care and protection during the past night, and we ask You now to let Your blessing rest upon us. Help us to begin the day with the solemn dedication of ourselves to Your service, and then to go to the duties of our several stations, with an earnest desire to do everything in Your fear, and with a view to Your glory.

We ask You, O Lord, to establish us in the great doctrines of Your gospel; may we be grounded in the faith of Christ crucified for us; may that history which we read in Your holy Word, of our Savior's coming down from heaven, to live as our example and to die as the atonement for our sins, affect us deeply, and have its full influence upon us. May it excite our warmest gratitude to Him who died for us; may it inspire us with hatred against sin; may it help us to rise above the fear of wick-

67

ed men; and may we learn to identify with our suffering and despised Lord. May that zeal to save us, which He showed, awaken in each of us a concern for our own salvation; and may it be the chief desire of our hearts to be made partakers of all the benefits both of His death and of His glorious resurrection.

But since we are by nature so prone to evil, and so little disposed to spiritual things, we ask You, O God, to purify our minds from all sinful and vain desires, by the powerful working of Your grace. O Lord, grant unto us the power of Your Holy Spirit. May He dwell within us, as a spirit of purity and holiness, a spirit of truth and of wisdom, of peace also, and love, and of holy joy, and consolation. May we pass this day in the thankful remembrance of Your mercies and in the diligent performance of Your commandments. May no evil thoughts, no angry tempers, no distressing doubts or fears disturb us. May we serve You our God, and live peaceably with all men. May we be kind and humble, patient and thankful; and sober-minded, and temperate in all things. May we fulfill the duties of the day; and may we lie down at night, praising You again for all Your goodness; and committing ourselves with holy confidence to Your mercy.

We ask these blessings in the name of Jesus Christ, our only mediator. Amen.

OUR FATHER in heaven, hallowed be Your name. Your kingdom come. Your will be done on earth as it is in heaven. Give us this day our daily bread. And forgive us our debts, as we forgive our debtors. And do not lead us into temptation, but deliver us from the evil one. For Yours is the kingdom, and the power, and the glory, forever. Amen.

MEMORY VERSE

"When He, the Spirit of truth, has come, He will guide you into all truth; for He will not speak on His own authority, but whatever He hears He will speak; and He will tell you things to come" (John 16:13).

EVENING PRAYER

LORD, our heavenly Father, almighty and most merciful God, we are gathered together to offer as a Christian family our united prayers and supplications to You. You understand the secrets of all our hearts. You have known all the circumstances of our past lives and are acquainted with the present attitudes of all our minds. You know whether we are of the number of those who live in forgetfulness of You and persist in their stubborn ways, not seeing their danger; or whether we are of that happy number who have embraced Your gospel with true contrition of heart and have obeyed its solemn call to repentance and newness of life.

O Lord, do not allow that any of us should harden our hearts against You. May we fear, lest death should overtake us in our sins. But, if any of us have already received Your truth in the love of your lasting peace, if any of us have already repented truly of our sins, and begun to lead a new life, and to walk in the way of Your commandments, we pray that we may learn to follow them fully to the end.

O Lord, how great is the privilege of those who can look up with holy confidence to You. How blessed are they who have You for their friend, You who made heaven and earth and have all things under Your government. We ask You to receive us into Your favor; to adopt us into Your family; and to make all things work together for our good.

Having sought, first, the kingdom of God and His righteousness, may all other things be added unto us. May Your merciful providence direct the events of our lives. May Your arm be stretched out to protect us. May Your Spirit sustain and strengthen us; and, if it should please You to send us trials and afflictions, may Your grace sanctify all our sorrows and cause them to be an instrument of our eternal benefit.

We now commit ourselves to You for this night; earnestly asking You to pardon our sins and to take us under Your gracious protection. May we rise in the morning with every good desire welling up in us, and go to the duties of the following day, remembering that we are candidates for a heavenly prize. May we now look beyond these temporal things to a better and more enduring inheritance.

We offer up these our imperfect prayers in the name of our Lord and Savior, Jesus Christ. Amen.

*T*HE grace of the Lord Jesus Christ, and the love of God, and the communion of the Holy Spirit be with you all. Amen.

MORNING PRAYER

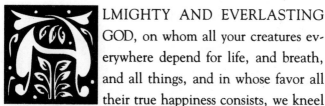LMIGHTY AND EVERLASTING
GOD, on whom all your creatures ev-
erywhere depend for life, and breath,
and all things, and in whose favor all
their true happiness consists, we kneel
down to acknowledge the author of our being. We, Your
creatures whom Your hand has made and whom Your
bounty has supported, kneel to pray for Your blessing
upon us.

We are sorry that we are by nature so prone to evil
and that, amidst the many gifts given to us, we so seldom lift up our thoughts to Him who is the giver. Every
night You again refresh us with sleep; and every morning, You renew Your various mercies to us, giving us
health, and strength, and talents for Your service, and
provide to us fresh opportunities for our usefulness in the
world.

We pray that, as our days pass away, we may be improving the time that is allotted to us. May we gather wisdom from Your sacred Word. May we diligently attend to the means of grace; and may we labor, each of us, as Your faithful servants, in our various callings.

We ask You to impress upon us a deep sense of the importance of eternity. May we be looking continually to the end of our course; and, remembering how soon all in which we here delight shall pass away forever, may we prepare to give our account of all things done in the body. Day by day may we have our conversation in heaven, moderating our affections towards the things of this world and living here below a life of faith in the Son of God.

And now, O Lord, whatever the employment that You have allotted to us, may we fulfill it as in Your fear, and with a view to Your glory. And wherever we are this day, be present with us to bless us. May Your Spirit enlighten, strengthen, and direct us. May we fall into no sin nor run into any kind of danger. We pray, especially, for grace to conquer those sins that most easily beset us. You know, O Lord, our many infirmities. Give us grace to be careful and circumspect. Let us avoid every approach to our former temptations, and let us renew our repentance with true sorrow and contrition of heart.

Hear us, we now beseech You, in these our imperfect supplications. Forgive us all our past transgressions; and grant us grace for the time to come. We ask all for the sake of Jesus Christ our Lord. Amen.

OUR FATHER in heaven, hallowed be Your name. Your kingdom come. Your will be done on earth as it is in heaven. Give us this day our daily bread. And forgive us our debts, as we forgive our debtors. And do not lead us into temptation, but deliver us from the evil one. For Yours is the kingdom, and the power, and the glory, forever. Amen.

MEMORY VERSE

"Do not love the world or the things that are in the world. If anyone loves the world, the love of the Father is not in him" (1 John 2:15).

EVENING PRAYER

LORD ALMIGHTY, You are the God of our lives, the author of all our happiness, and the only source from which we can derive any true consolation and hope. You have declared in Your Word that You hear the prayers of Your creatures, and are rich in mercy to all who devoutly call upon You. Thus encouraged by Your gracious promises, we sinners, hopeless in ourselves and exposed to Your just condemnation, presume to call upon Your name and to implore Your blessing and Your mercy.

We confess that we have all trespassed against You. We have sinned by our ignoring of You; our iniquities have advanced with our advancing years; and if we now attempt to recollect all the evil that we have done, we are ashamed by the great number of our offenses. We confess that we have been vain and worldly, proud and self-willed. Though we have professed the Christian faith, we have continued too much engrossed by the present world, and too thoughtless of eternity. We have been inclined to cherish delusive hopes of much earthly good. Eager also for a favorable reputation with our fellow-creatures, we have shown little eagerness to please You.

We are sorry especially that though Your gospel has been preached to us, we have heard it with much indifference. We lament that, even with the powerful nature of its doctrines, we have been so little affected by it. Instead, often we have refused to follow Your will and the teachings of Christ, choosing to live according to the will of men and the corrupt behavior of this sinful world. O Lord, grant that we may not remain unresponsive to Your mercies in Jesus Christ. May we lie down this night deeply moved by the importance of eternity; and resolved to give up our future lives to that God who made us, and to that Savior who has redeemed us by His most precious blood.

We desire, also, to thank You for Your many temporal gifts. Blessed be Your name for all the mercies that we have experienced this day: our health and strength, our food and clothes, the various benefits and comforts of this mortal life. We are not worthy, O Lord, of the least of all Your gifts. And as we enjoy these earthly blessings, may we look forward, with cheerful and humble hope, to those greater things, which, as yet, eye has not seen, nor the ear heard, nor has it entered into the heart of man to conceive.

Accept, for our Savior's sake, whatever we may have done this day in any measure according to Your commands; and receive these our imperfect prayers, that we offer in His name. Amen.

THE grace of the Lord Jesus Christ, and the love of God, and the communion of the Holy Spirit be with you all. Amen.

MORNING PRAYER

LMIGHTY GOD, by whose will we were created, and by whose providence we have been sustained, give to us Your blessing this day. By Your mercy we have been called to the knowledge of our redeemer, and by Your grace we have thought or done whatever has been acceptable to You. Now by that grace strengthen us for the performance of the duties before us. And, since You have ordained labor to be the lot of man, and know the wants and necessities of all Your creatures, bless our many activities and employments.

Give us, this day, our daily bread. Feed us with food convenient for us. If it be Your pleasure to cause us to abound with the good things of this life, give us a compassionate spirit, that we may be ready to relieve the wants of others. But let neither riches nor poverty estrange our hearts from You, nor cause us to become negligent of those treasures in heaven that can never be taken from us. And into whatever circumstances of life we may be brought, teach us to be cheerful and content. In our affliction, let us remember how often we have been comforted; in our prosperity, may we acknowledge from whose hand our blessings are received.

And we ask You to help us to so remember our sins that we may be brought to true repentance, to sincere sorrow, and to contrition of soul. Strengthen our faith in Jesus Christ our Lord; and grant, that through the gracious help of Your Holy Spirit we may obtain that peace that the world cannot give. Enable us to pass the remainder of our lives in humble resignation and willing obedience.

We acknowledge, O God, that every day is Your gift and ought to be used according to Your command. You, in whose hands are life and death, and by whose mercy we are spared, help us so to improve the time, that we may every day become more holy in Your sight. And when it shall please You to call us from this mortal state, may we resign our souls into Your hands, with confidence and hope.

We commend to Your fatherly goodness all our relations and friends, especially those who are the most closely united to us. We ask You to look mercifully upon them; and to grant them whatever may most promote their present and eternal joy.

Bless the president of these United States, and all in authority. Extend Your goodness to our whole native land. Pity the sorrows and relieve the necessities of all mankind. And let Your kingdom come and Your will be done in earth, as it is in heaven.

O Lord, hear our prayers, for Jesus Christ's sake, to whom, with You and the Holy Ghost, be all honor and glory, world without end. Amen.

OUR FATHER in heaven, hallowed be Your name. Your kingdom come. Your will be done on earth as it is in heaven. Give us this day our daily bread. And forgive us our debts, as we forgive our debtors. And do not lead us into temptation, but deliver us from the evil one. For Yours is the kingdom, and the power, and the glory, forever. Amen.

MEMORY VERSE

"Peace I leave with you, my peace I give to you; not as the world gives do I give to you. Let not your heart be troubled neither, let it be afraid" (John 14:27).

EVENING PRAYER

O LORD GOD, our heavenly Father, we are gathered as a Christian family to thank You for the mercies of the past day and to implore Your blessing before we lie down to rest. We would ever remember the frailty of our nature and our utter uncertainty how long we may have to live. We are placed in this world for a short time and must soon enter into eternity. We must go to the Father of our spirits, and give account of all things done in the body, and must then receive our eternal judgment.

O may this solemn thought return to our minds with each new day: that we may begin our duties, reflecting on the ends for which we were born; and may lie down each night, examining whether we are so passing our time on earth as we shall wish we had done when we are about to die and to appear before Your judgment seat.

We ask You, O Lord, to give us a sacred jealousy over our condition, lest we fall short of our heavenly calling. May we learn to put our whole trust in You, and to place our delight in serving You. Pardon all our disobedience in the time past—our many negligences, as well as sins; the wasted time; the idle words; and the evil attitudes of this day.

We would lie down trusting in the merits of Jesus Christ our Lord, in whose gracious promises to every repenting sinner we place all our hope. And while we thus commend our souls to Your mercies in Christ, to You do we commit all our worldly affairs. In Your hand, O Lord, whose providence it is that brings every thing to pass, we leave the issue of all our undertakings; for You know better than ourselves what is for our good.

We ask You to bless us with all spiritual blessings and to sanctify to us the daily events of our lives. We ask You to lay upon us no greater burden than we are able to bear and to train us, by Your merciful goodness and Your tender care, for the performance of better services than we have yet rendered You in the world. We pray for strength against every temptation and for final victory over every sin. Arm us for every conflict; fit us for every duty that we have to fulfill. Let us diligently perform our work in life. Let us, at the same time, live in peace and love, and grow in all offices of kindness to each other.

O Lord, unite us as one Christian family together. May we be partakers of the same faith and heirs of the same hope. May our united prayers continually ascend to the throne of Your heavenly grace, and may Your blessing rest upon us.

Hear us, we ask You, in these our humble supplications, for Jesus Christ our Savior's sake. Amen.

THE grace of the Lord Jesus Christ, and the love of God, and the communion of the Holy Spirit be with you all. Amen.

MORNING PRAYER

OST GRACIOUS AND MERCIFUL GOD, who has protected us through the night and refreshed us with sleep, we offer our sincere thanks and praise for Your various and great mercies. We confess that we are unworthy to come into Your presence, before whom the angels veil their faces, and in whose sight the heavens are not clean; for our lives have been unholy, and our sins many and great. If, therefore, You should mark iniquity, O Lord, who shall stand?

But we rejoice that there is with You forgiveness and full redemption, through Jesus Christ Your Son. Pleading, therefore, His sacrifice, and trusting in His intercession, we approach the throne of Your grace and say, "God be merciful to us sinners, for Jesus Christ's sake." O Lord, grant to us true repentance and a lively faith. Convince us of our guilt. Show us everything (either in our hearts or lives) that has been displeasing to You.

We pray that, through faith in the blood of Your Son, we may obtain peace in our consciences. Through the blessed hope that is set before us, may we also be raised above the various troubles, disappointments, and temptations, of this present evil world.

We pray, also, that through the knowledge of Your truth, and the help of Your Spirit we may be disposed to fulfill every precept of Your Word. May we do unto all men as we would that they should do unto us; and may we forgive one another, even as we hope to be forgiven. May we be clothed with humility; and, denying all ungodliness and worldly lusts, may we live soberly, righteously, and godly in this present world. May we be content with such things as we have, fulfilling, each of us, our proper duties. May we watch against anger, malice, hatred, envy, and all other evil tempers, which are ready to rise up within us. And thus doing Your will, and walking in Your ways, and improving every talent committed to us, may we wait for the second coming of our Lord.

We also most humbly beseech You, O Father of mercies, to look down with an eye of favor on all our friends and relations.

Bring home to Your flock all those who are wandering in the ways of sin. Strengthen and confirm those who love Your name, that they may rejoice in Your salvation.

Be gracious unto all whom You have disposed to be kind to us; sanctify them to Yourself and shower down Your best blessings upon them. Pity those who are afflicted, tempted, persecuted, enslaved, or oppressed; and in Your good time give them deliverance.

Give success to the labors of the ministers of your gospel. Bless and purify Your church. Have compassion on our native land; and, though many sins testify against us, take not away Your grace so long afforded us.

Bless the president of these United States, and all in authority; direct the public measures to our best interests, and to Your glory; and teach all people to serve their generation according to Your will. And grant that all the changes in the kingdoms of the world may further Your glory, and in the furtherance of Your gospel.

These, and all other things needful for us, we ask in the name of Jesus Christ our Lord. Amen.

O*UR FATHER in heaven, hallowed be Your name. Your kingdom come. Your will be done on earth as it is in heaven. Give us this day our daily bread. And forgive us our debts, as we forgive our debtors. And do not lead us into temptation, but deliver us from the evil one. For Yours is the kingdom, and the power, and the glory, forever. Amen.*

MEMORY VERSE

"For the grace of God that brings salvation has appeared to all men, teaching us that, denying ungodliness and worldly lusts, we should live soberly, righteously, and godly in this present age" (Titus 2:11-12).

EVENING PRAYER

GOD, who through Your tender mercy did send Your Son Jesus Christ into the world to die for our sins, we ask You to bestow upon us all those abundant blessings that, through Him, You have provided for the children of men. Numberless are our wants, and we would, therefore, daily increase in supplication and prayer. We ask You to bestow upon us all things that You know to be needful for us, to carry us in safety through this life, and to bring us to the end of our days in peace. We ask You to protect us in all dangers, to guide us in all our difficulties, to sustain us in all our temptations and trials, and to lay upon us no greater burden than we are able to bear. We ask You to support us with Your heavenly grace, to strengthen our faith, to animate our hope, and to enlarge our charity. We ask You to impress upon us every doctrine of Your gospel, and thus to purify our hearts.

We thank You, heavenly Father, that for us sinners You have provided the blessing of salvation. May we submit all our affairs to the merciful God, who, having rescued our souls from destruction, and shown us the path of life, has promised also that all things shall work together for good to them who love Him.

And, while we trust You, let us also diligently obey You. Whatever things are true, are honest, are lovely, and are of good report, may we meditate on these things. Fill us, O Lord, with compassion to our fellow creatures, even as You have had compassion on us. Give us hearts to deny ourselves, and to be kind and generous to others, always remembering that it is more blessed to give than to receive.

We ask You to give us tender consciences, that we may flee from all evil. We desire, as much as is possible in this state of trial, to be kept in paths of safety. We ask not for wealth, reputation, honor, or prosperity, but we pray for a calm and peaceful spirit, for every opportunity of leading a holy life, and for such circumstances in this world as may be most free from temptation. We pray for Your preserving grace, for holiness of life, and for eternal salvation at the last day.

Pardon, we now ask You, all the sins of the past day; we repent sincerely of the evil that we have done and, also, of our neglect of the good that we might have done. We implore both the pardon of our sins and the acceptance of our imperfect services, in the name of our only Lord and Savior, Jesus Christ. Amen.

*T*HE grace of the Lord Jesus Christ, and the love of God, and the communion of the Holy Spirit be with you all. Amen.

DAY 14

MORNING PRAYER

LMIGHTY AND EVERLASTING GOD, the giver of all good things, we, Your creatures, desire to offer our deep thanks for all Your temporal as well as spiritual mercies. We bless You for our creation, preservation, and all the blessings of this life, but above all for Your inestimable love in the redemption of the world by our Lord Jesus Christ. We thank You that the knowledge of this salvation has extended to us, and that we have been instructed in the will of God and in the blessed doctrines of Your gospel. We praise You for that good providence that has directed our steps in life. We thank You for the times You have enlightened our minds to understand the truths that we have heard, and to know the things that make for our everlasting peace.

We now most humbly ask You, O Lord, grant that we may not walk in darkness; but as He who has called us is holy, may we also be holy in all manner of conversation. Give us grace to overcome our sinful appetites and passions, and to be sober and temperate in all things. Assist us, also, by your Holy Spirit to subdue the corrupt affections of the mind: all anger, malice, envy, pride, and covetousness. Make us patient and contented, kind and charitable, humble and spiritually minded. We pray You also to make us diligent and useful in that world in which You have placed us. May we not misspend our time, nor neglect any opportunity of doing good, but may we be willing daily to deny ourselves, that we may the more abundantly minister to the various wants of others.

We ask You, O Lord, to give unto each of us grace to know the several duties to which we are called; and to be both faithful and zealous in the performance of them.

May those in authority in this house remember that they are only the stewards of the good things that You entrust to them, and that they must give account hereafter to their Master who is in heaven. Give to the children of this family grace to be obedient in all things, to learn to walk in the fear of the Lord, and to exercise brotherly kindness toward each other. May others in this house remember that Your eye is upon them and that the gospel, which they have been taught, requires them not only to approve themselves to their authorities in the flesh, but also to please God who tries the heart.

May we all live together in Christian peace, harmony, and love. May we seek to minister to each other's comfort, to bear each other's burdens, and to promote each other's temporal as well as spiritual good. Teach us, also, to abound in charity toward all those with whom we may this day have any contact.

Pardon, we ask You, for Christ's sake, the large number of our past negligences and sins, and help us to awake to righteousness, and to be diligent in every good work. When we shall lie down tonight, may we have the testimony of our consciences, that we have been serving You according to our best opportunities and abilities, with humility and integrity of heart.

We pray for your blessing on our president and country, on our friends and relations, and on all who are afflicted in mind, body, or circumstances. Have pity on those who are walking in the way of their own hearts and bring them home, O Lord, to Your flock.

Pardon the coldness and imperfection of these our prayers; and accept them for Your Son our Lord Jesus Christ's sake. Amen.

O*UR FATHER in heaven, hallowed be Your name. Your kingdom come. Your will be done on earth as it is in heaven. Give us this day our daily bread. And forgive us our debts, as we forgive our debtors. And do not lead us into temptation, but deliver us from the evil one. For Yours is the kingdom, and the power, and the glory, forever. Amen.*

MEMORY VERSE

"Let all bitterness, wrath, anger, clamor and evil speaking be put away from you, with all malice" (Ephesians 4:31).

EVENING PRAYER

LORD GOD, our heavenly Father, whose mercies are over all Your works, and who has, on this day, supplied our returning wants, we render thanks to You for all the bounties of Your provi-dence; and we desire now to lie down under a deep sense both of our own unworthiness and of Your unspeakable goodness.

We adore You, especially for the gift of Jesus Christ, Your Son, through whom we have pardon of our sins and the gift of everlasting life. We are all sinners in Your sight and are exposed to Your just condemnation; but though our offenses have abounded, yet Your grace has still more increased through Jesus Christ.

We desire to confess and lament the sins of the day now past. Forgive, O Lord, all our negligences, as well as our more blatant offenses. Forgive all our evil thoughts, words, and works. We would lament every misspent hour and every neglected opportunity of doing good. We regret our lack of love to You our God, and our lack of zeal in Your service. We regret, also, the great imperfection of our charity toward those around us. You have commanded us to love our neighbor as ourselves, but we are continually seeking our own interest, indulging our own ease, and consulting our own feelings. Help us, we ask You, to follow the example of our blessed Savior, who did not please Himself but went about doing good; He has commanded us to continually deny ourselves, take up our cross, and follow Him.

We ask You to bless to us the events of this day. We would remember that all things are directed by Your unerring wisdom, and that they shall work together for good to those who love You. May any trial that we have experienced this day teach us more and more to know ourselves; may every sorrow wean us from this present world; and may every enjoyment be the means of stirring our gratitude to You, the author of all good. May the afflictions of others call forth our Christian sympathy and make us abundant in the exercises of our charity.

We pray for Your blessing on all our friends and relations. Guard them from evil by night and by day and especially from whatsoever may hurt their souls. Establish them in Your true faith and make them fruitful in good works. Bestow Your special blessing on the rising generation.

May the children of this family live in Your fear and maintain Your cause in the world. May they receive the truths taught them into an honest heart and be ever followers of that which is good.

Bless our rulers and country. Give grace to all ministers of Your gospel. Have pity on the poor and the afflicted, and make it the daily business of all our lives to minister to the sorrows and wants of others and to increase in every good work.

We present these our humble and imperfect supplications, in the name of our Lord and Savior, Jesus Christ. Amen.

*T*HE *grace of the Lord Jesus Christ, and the love of God, and the communion of the Holy Spirit be with you all. Amen.*

MORNING PRAYER

GREAT AND ETERNAL BEING, God of all power and might, giver of every good and perfect gift, and author of all our mercies, we kneel down, imploring You to bestow Your protection and blessing on this family. Through the bountiful goodness of our heavenly Father, we have been favored with innumerable mercies, and we would humbly thank You for them. But we ask You to add to all our other blessings the forgiveness of our sins through faith in that Savior whom You have revealed to us in the gospel.

In addition, we ask You to impress deeply on our minds, through the power of Your Holy Spirit, the great doctrines of Your Word. Give us a clear perception of the evil of sin, a deep conviction of our own guilt, a solemn belief in heaven and hell, and a true sense of our obligations to the Lord who bought us. We who bear the name Christian and know the truths of the gospel should not live in the same manner as unbelievers; therefore enable us, by applying those heart-affecting doctrines that we have learned, to become distinguished as the disciples of Jesus Christ our Lord. May we indeed cleave to the Lord, with full purpose of heart, being pure in our most secret thoughts and imaginations. We desire to suppress those high and self-exalting thoughts that are so apt to rise up within us. Remind us constantly of how we owe everything that we have or hope for to Your bountiful goodness and to Your mercies in Christ Jesus.

And being supported by Your grace and grounded in the faith of Christ crucified for us, we pray that we may be enabled to practice every good work. May we be just and true in all our dealings, doing unto others as we wish that they should do unto us. May we be humble, thankful, and contented; and may we do honor to Your gospel by the manifestation of every Christian grace.

Give us grace to maintain a constant battle with all evil. May we ourselves avoid every approach to it; and may we attempt, according to our opportunities and ability, to persuade all those over whom we have any influence to keep at the greatest distance from temptation. O Lord, enable us to show that we are Christians not only in general profession but in all sincerity and seriousness. May we be strict and self-denying, yet kind and liberal to others, honest and charitable, compassionate and courteous. Teach us to understand Your abounding grace in the gospel, that we may ourselves abound in every work of charity. Enable us to find favor in the sight of those around us, and especially of those who are dearest to us, so that we may improve our influence, for their benefit in this life, and for the furtherance of their everlasting salvation.

Bless us, O Lord, in these Christian purposes, for from You alone comes the strength to serve You, and to You we would continually look up. Hear us, we ask You, in these our supplications; and grant to us the help of Your Holy Spirit, that we may live this day according to these our prayers, and that all the fruits of holiness may abound in us.

We ask every blessing in the name of Jesus Christ. Amen.

*O*UR FATHER *in heaven, hallowed be Your name. Your kingdom come. Your will be done on earth as it is in heaven. Give us this day our daily bread. And forgive us our debts, as we forgive our debtors. And do not lead us into temptation, but deliver us from the evil one. For Yours is the kingdom, and the power, and the glory, forever. Amen.*

MEMORY VERSE

"Every good gift and every perfect gift is from above, and comes down from the Father of lights, with whom there is no variation or shadow of turning" (James 1:17).

EVENING PRAYER

LORD GOD, our Heavenly Father, we ask You now to deliver us from all wandering thoughts and to enable us to worship You in an acceptable manner, through Jesus Christ our Lord.

We ask You to pardon all the sins of this day. We confess that we have not served You as we ought, but we desire to repent of both our negligences and our sins; and we would seriously resolve that, by Your grace assisting us, we will seek continually to improve our lives, and to walk more closely to the precepts of Your holy Word.

Pardon whatever pride or vanity we have this day indulged, whatever angry words we have spoken, and whatever sinful thoughts we have harbored in our minds. Forgive our want of sufficient tenderness of conscience in the performance of those duties in which we have been engaged. Pardon, especially, that want of love both to You and to our fellow creatures, which causes us to live so much to ourselves, and to do so little either for the benefit of others, or for Your glory.

We ask You, O Lord, to give us hearts more devoted to You and more dead to sin, as well as to all the things of this world. Teach us to know how frail is our life, how short may be the time of our journey here, and how serious may be the account that we shall have to give of all things done in the body, as soon as we shall be called to eternity. Let us lie down, night after night, as those who know not whether they may lie down to rise no more. May we repent daily of our sins and then be accepted in You through Jesus Christ our Lord; and may we resolve, by Your grace assisting us, to bring forth all those fruits of righteousness, which are by Him, to the praise and glory of God. Save us from a barren and unfruitful faith, by which we miserably deceive our own souls. Give us that true peace of mind that they alone possess who love Your law, and save us from that hope of the hypocrite, which shall perish when God takes away his soul. May we live a life of purity and holiness, of watchfulness and self-denial, and of diligence in every good work.

O Lord, take us now under Your care, both pardoning our sins and accepting our imperfect services on the past day.

We implore Your special protection on the children of this family. Save them from the temptations of this vain and evil world. Watch over them during the weakness and inexperience of their youth, and prepare them for the duties to which Your providence shall call them.

And bless with us all others who are dear to us; and make us to lie down in perfect charity with all men.

We ask every blessing in the name and through the merits of the great mediator and intercessor, Jesus Christ our Lord. Amen.

THE grace of the Lord Jesus Christ, and the love of God, and the communion of the Holy Spirit be with you all. Amen.

MORNING PRAYER

 LORD GOD ALMIGHTY, who has made the world and all things in it, in whose favor is life, and in whose displeasure is misery, we kneel down, asking You to strengthen our faith in all the promises and threatenings of Your Word. May we live as those who know themselves to be frail and dying creatures on the brink of an awesome eternity.

We bless You for having brought life and immortality to light by the gospel. We thank You that Your Son has died and risen again, has broken the bonds of death, and has opened to us the gates of everlasting life. We thank You for the glorious hopes held out to each believer in His name; and at the same time we would rejoice with trembling, remembering the condemnation that belongs to the despisers of His gospel, and to all who receive this grace of God in vain.

O Lord, grant unto us faith in that eternal world to which we are hastening. May we realize these unseen things; may we turn from the love of this vain world; may we perceive the sin that dwells in us and the evil that lies around us, and be looking forward to that blessed time when we shall put away the body of this death and dwell forever with the Lord.

Give us grace to follow the faith and patience of Your saints, who turned from sin to follow God and who endured even to the end, whose hearts were estranged from things below, and whose affections were set on things above. They went through trials, persecutions, and a great number of afflictions, because they counted Christ worthy of all obedience and able to finally save and deliver them. May we, who have the example of their faith, be willing to deny ourselves, take up our cross, and follow Christ; not living an idle, careless life, while we call ourselves the followers of them who now inherit the promises. May we daily mortify the body of sin, and daily renew the conflict with our spiritual enemies. May we be looking continually to Jesus, the author and finisher of our faith; who, for the joy set before Him, endured the cross, despising the shame, and now is seated at the right hand of God.

May we be so enlivened by our Christian faith as to be willing cheerfully to endure the evils of life and to submit to all Your righteous will concerning us. If there be any of us who are still strangers to You, teach us to remember how short and uncertain are all our days on earth. Or if there be any of us who are indolent and materialistic, too much occupied with this present world, raise our thoughts to those things that are above, that we may be fellow citizens with Your saints and with the household of God. May we all give diligence to make our calling and election sure: may we all repent, and forsake our sins, and believe in Christ; may we all die daily to the things of time, and rise to newness of life; may we all pass through things temporal, so that we do not lose the things eternal.

We ask every blessing in the name of Jesus Christ our Lord. Amen.

OUR FATHER in heaven, hallowed be Your name. Your kingdom come. Your will be done on earth as it is in heaven. Give us this day our daily bread. And forgive us our debts, as we forgive our debtors. And do not lead us into temptation, but deliver us from the evil one. For Yours is the kingdom, and the power, and the glory, forever. Amen.

MEMORY VERSE

"And He said to them all, 'If any man desires to come after me, let him deny himself, and take up his cross daily and follow Me'" (Luke 9:23).

EVENING PRAYER

ETERNAL GOD, Father of men and angels, who has established the heavens and the earth in a wonderful order, causing day and night to succeed each other, we make our humble address to Your divine majesty, begging Your mercy and protection, this night and forever.

O Lord, pardon all our sins, our light and rash words, the vanity and impurity of our thoughts, our unjust and unkind actions, and whatever we have done wrong this day or at any time before. O God, our souls are troubled through the remembrance of our past transgressions, and we are daily exposed, through the frailty and sinfulness of our natures, to every new temptation. Of ourselves we are not able to resist. We, therefore, earnestly beg of you to give us a great portion of Your grace, such as may be sufficient and effective for the death of all our corruptions, so that, as we have formerly served sinful desires, now we may give up ourselves to Your service, in all the duties of a holy life.

Teach us to walk always as in Your presence; and put into our souls great love to You, that it may become our chief work to promote Your glory, and to root out all habits of sin; so that, in faith and purity, we may wait patiently for the coming of our Lord Jesus.

Into Your hands we now commend ourselves, asking You to so bless and sanctify our sleep to us that it may be a refreshment to our wearied bodies and so your blessing may enable us the better to serve You. And whether we sleep or wake, live or die, may we be Your servants.

We also ask You, O God, to send down Your blessing on all our dear friends and relations. Bless them individually, in their families, and in all their undertakings; and cause them to advance Your honor, and to live to Your glory.

Be a father and a friend to the children of this family. Let Your providence lead them through the dangers, and temptations, and ignorance of their youth, that they may not run into foolishness, nor give way to any unrestrained appetite. Be pleased so to order the events of their lives, that, by a good education, by prudent counsel, and by Your restraining grace, they may be trained up to serve You in the midst of an evil generation; and, after a useful and holy life may come to a peaceful and happy death, and may be made heirs with Christ in the glories of His heavenly kingdom.

Look down with an eye of favor on the whole church of Christ. Have compassion on Your afflicted servants. Give them increase of faith, patience, and hope; and, in Your good time, give them deliverance.

And, You who wills not the death of a sinner, have pity on the many who walk not in obedience to your commandments. Turn them from all their sins, so that their souls may be saved in the day of Jesus Christ. Support also the weak; establish the doubtful and wavering; help the tempted; and raise up those who are fallen. And teach us all to have compassion on the infirmities of our brethren and to act charitably one toward another.

Hear, O Lord, these and all our prayers, for the sake of Your only Son Jesus Christ, our Mediator and Redeemer. Amen.

*T*HE *grace of the Lord Jesus Christ, and the love of God, and the communion of the Holy Spirit be with you all. Amen.*

MORNING PRAYER

LORD ALMIGHTY, who are merciful and gracious, patient, and of great goodness, we approach You as the God of mercy, imploring You to hear these our prayers and to pardon the multitude of our sins, for the sake of Jesus Christ. Day after day, we add to the number of our transgressions: every night we have the sins of the preceding day to repent of; and every morning we have reason to fear unless we should again yield to temptation and return to our former iniquities. We pray, therefore, for Your preserving and protecting grace. O Lord, put Your Spirit into all our hearts, that we, being made pure and holy in our secret thoughts, may not fail to perform all that is good and acceptable in Your sight.

Dispose each of us on this day to employ regularly our many talents in Your service. While we pursue the various duties of our calling, may we have a single eye to

Your glory, and may we undertake no employment on which we cannot hope for Your blessing. Give us such a portion of Your grace, O Lord, that we may desire to do not only that which is in some degree beneficial but that which is most excellent and most completely useful. May no spirit of self-indulgence, no love of ease, no dread of opposition, and no fear of shame prevent our placing our lives heartily in Your service. Make us willing in all respects to deny ourselves, that we may live to You. Teach us to enter into the spirit of those Christians and apostles of old, who counted not their lives dear to themselves so that they might finish their course with joy, and who rejoiced that they were counted worthy to suffer shame for the name of Christ. Living in unity and godly love, they were seen striving together for the faith of the gospel, not terrified in any way by their adversaries.

Grant unto every member of this family Your peace, and all Your heavenly consolations. Make us to be of one heart and one mind, praising You for Your mercies, praying to You for Your grace, and uniting in the confession of our daily sins before You.

Establish us in Your faith, fear, and love; and enlighten us, that we may understand Your whole will concerning us. Where we have erred, have pity on our mistakes; and if we have wandered from the right way, we implore You in mercy bring us back. Lead us, O Lord, into the paths of righteousness and peace. And, if we have in any measure attained to the knowledge of Your truth, may we bring our faith into active exercise. May we watch our hearts, and bridle our tongues, and govern our tempers. May we be ready to forgive, even as we hope to be forgiven. May we be steadfast, and immoveable, always abounding in the work of the Lord, knowing that our labor shall not be in vain in the Lord.

We now commit ourselves to You for this day. Help us to live according to these prayers, and thus may we be prepared for Your heavenly kingdom. We ask this for our Savior's sake. Amen.

OUR FATHER in heaven, hallowed be Your name. Your kingdom come. Your will be done on earth as it is in heaven. Give us this day our daily bread. And forgive us our debts, as we forgive our debtors. And do not lead us into temptation, but deliver us from the evil one. For Yours is the kingdom, and the power, and the glory, forever. Amen.

MEMORY VERSE

"Therefore, my beloved brethren, be steadfast, immoveable, always abounding in the work of the Lord, for you know that your labor is not in vain in the Lord" (1 Corinthians 15:58).

EVENING PRAYER

LMIGHTY AND EVER BLESSED GOD, who preserves our lives, and sustains our health and strength, and multiplies our comforts and enjoyments, we are gathered together to praise You for the mercies that we have experienced since we were last assembled to worship Your holy name. You are the author of all good; without You, we are utterly weak and helpless, as well as miserable. O Lord, continue to give us Your gracious care and preserve us this night, both in body and soul, from every evil.

We ask You, especially, to grant to us all the pardon of sin, and a cheerful confidence in Your favor, through Jesus Christ our Lord. Give us peace through His atoning blood; and being thus reconciled to You our God, may we also be in charity with all men. Take from us, O Lord, every angry passion, as well as every tormenting fear of Your wrath. We ask You, also, to deliver us from those anxieties and cares that are too apt to distress our minds. Let us trust Your gracious providence; and ever commit ourselves and all our concerns to You, as to a wise and faithful Creator, and as Father and friend in Christ.

Bless us, we ask You, to the end of our lives. Support us in all our future trials, guide us in all our difficulties, strengthen us for the several duties of our stations, and sustain us in sorrow, sickness, and adversity in this mortal life.

We ask You to bless our friends and relations. Deliver them from all the dangers and sorrows of this evil world; and save them, especially, from sin. Unite them with us in the bonds of a common faith so that we may all be members of the same blessed family above.

Have compassion on the children of this house, fill them with the knowledge of Your will; and give them grace to serve You, without fear, in holiness and righteousness all the days of their lives.

Have mercy on our president. Direct the councils of this nation. Bless our courts. Inspire our clergy with the spirit of true religion. Give to the poor, contentment with their lot; and to the rich, a spirit of compassion and kindness. Extend Your goodness to all mankind. Put an end to war and discord, as well as to vice and superstition; and send Your gospel over the earth, to enlighten those who still sit in darkness and in the shadow of death.

These prayers we would humbly present, with one heart and one mind, at the throne of Your heavenly grace; and we ask You to hear and answer them, according to the riches of Your mercy in Jesus Christ. Amen.

*T*HE *grace of the Lord Jesus Christ, and the love of God, and the communion of the Holy Spirit be with you all. Amen.*

MORNING PRAYER

OST MERCIFUL AND GRACIOUS GOD, we kneel down to thank You for Your protection and care during the past night. And we now lift up our voice unto You in the morning, imploring You this day to bless us, watching over us by Your merciful providence and delivering us from all evil.

We are prone, O Lord, to fall into sin. How many incidents arise every day, that draw forth our natural corruptions. Therefore, we ask You, who knows our frame and foresees the trials that come upon us, to prepare us for them. Enable us, amidst the various difficulties, temptations, and sorrows of life, to walk as the patient followers of Christ, and as the faithful servants of the Most High God.

We bless You, O God, for all Your goodness to us in times past: for every trial You have lightened, for every difficulty and snare You have taken out of our way, and for every affliction that You have either sanctified or removed.

We thank You that we are here meeting together, in so much peace and comfort, to offer up our praises to You. We thank You for all Your unnumbered mercies; for our health and strength, and all our worldly goods; for our friends and kind benefactors; and we pray that we may, each of us in our stations, be instruments in Your hand for the benefit of our fellow-creatures. At the same time, we desire to be faithful witnesses in the world of the truth and excellency of Your gospel.

O Lord, grant that this day we may walk in a manner worthy of our great obligations to You, and of our high and heavenly calling. May we remember both Your spiritual and temporal mercies, and be occupied in acts of grateful obedience to You. And we ask You to impress upon us more deeply those truths of Your gospel that prepare us for every good and beneficent work. May we think of the Savior who died on the cross for us, who endured all the extremities of misery that we might be saved, and is now at Your right hand making intercession for us. May we remember our Christian profession, living as believers in this crucified Lord, deeply affected with the remembrance of His death and His glorious resurrection. May we all die to sin and live to righteousness; and, as He who has called us is holy, may we also be holy in all manner of conversation. We pray, O Lord, for Your protection this day. May we faithfully follow

Him whose name we bear; may we have hope in His mercy; and may we finally enter into His glory. Amen.

O UR FATHER *in heaven, hallowed be Your name. Your kingdom come. Your will be done on earth as it is in heaven. Give us this day our daily bread. And forgive us our debts, as we forgive our debtors. And do not lead us into temptation, but deliver us from the evil one. For Yours is the kingdom, and the power, and the glory, forever. Amen.*

MEMORY VERSE

"[The Son] being the brightness of His glory and the express image of His person, and upholding all things by the word of His power, when He had by Himself purged our sins, sat down at the right hand of the Majesty on high" (Hebrews 1:3).

EVENING PRAYER

LORD, God Almighty, who hears the prayers of all who devoutly call upon Your name, we kneel down to make our supplications unto You this night. We implore You to take us under Your protection and to pardon, also, every sin that we may have committed against You this day.

At the same time, we ask You to impress upon us the importance of eternal things. May we be deeply persuaded, through the powerful help of Your Holy Spirit, that we can never prize our salvation too highly, nor strive too earnestly or unceasingly after it. Teach us to remember that we are dying creatures, who must soon enter into eternity, when we must either rise to a state of immortal happiness or sink into everlasting despair. May we never forget that one thing is needful; and may we, in comparison, despise all the things of this world, while we think of that better inheritance that can never be taken from us.

And pour out upon us, we ask You, the spirit of wisdom and of a sound mind. Deliver us from every error by which we may be in danger of being deceived. Convince us of the evil that has been hidden in our hearts, and of the many sins that we have committed. And bestow upon us deep repentance for them. At the same time, grant us such a lively faith in our Lord Jesus Christ that we may be comforted by the hope of His pardoning mercy and may be encouraged in pursuing our Christian course.

We would also implore You, as the God of providence, to show grace upon our various needs. Send us, we ask You, such circumstances in life, such degrees of health, such friends, and such opportunities of instruction, as may promote the edification and salvation of our souls. May Your Holy Spirit dwell within us, and may all things that influence us be ordered by You for our good. And may we see and acknowledge Your hand, both in Your chastisement, and in Your mercies. May we be enabled always to say, "It is the Lord who gives, and the Lord who takes away; blessed be the name of the Lord."

We commit ourselves to Your mercy and protection, for this night; and we desire to lie down at peace with You, and in perfect charity with all men.

And now, O Lord, if we have this day, misused our time, have forgotten You, or have in any way sinned against You, we here implore Your pardon, in the name of Jesus Christ.

We present these and all our prayers through the merits, and intercession of the same Blessed Savior. Amen.

THE grace of the Lord Jesus Christ, and the love of God, and the communion of the Holy Spirit be with you all. Amen.

MORNING PRAYER

LORD, God Almighty, our creator, preserver, and benefactor, we desire to thank You for all your past mercies; at the same time asking You to give us Your continual grace and to pour down Your blessing upon us.

We ask You to conduct us by Your merciful providence in our passage through this life. Defend us amidst our many dangers, deliver us from every trial, and order all the circumstances that affect us so that we may not be overpowered with difficulties, nor overwhelmed with temptations, which may come upon us when we are unprepared.

Preserve us, O Lord, from day to day, and from year to year. Give us grace to hate sin and to avoid those societies and employments that would lead our hearts away from You. May our eyes be opened to see the wickedness around us; and may we carefully abstain from all conformity to the sinful customs of this evil world. But when we reflect on the many hindrances to our leading a Christian life, when we contemplate temptations both from within and from without, when we look back to the past instances of our weakness, and forward to the yet untried scenes of danger and of difficulty; on You, O Lord, and on You alone, are we led to trust. Therefore, to You alone we lift up our daily prayer for grace to preserve us in the paths of righteousness, so that we may end our days in peace.

O Lord, grant unto us, this day, Your Holy Spirit. Keep alive in our souls the sense of spiritual things. Impress us with a recollection of the great truths that we have been taught. Fill us with a knowledge of those doctrines of Your gospel, which You have appointed to be the means of delivering man from sin and of preserving him in the ways of holiness, in the midst of an ungodly world.

Enable us to walk worthy of the Lord throughout the day that is now before us. May we be obedient to your will, submissive to Your providence, and ever thankful for Your mercies.

Hear, O Lord, and answer these our prayers. Forgive also our numberless transgressions, and accept our imperfect services, for Your mercies' sake in Jesus Christ our Lord. Amen.

OUR FATHER in heaven, hallowed be Your name. Your kingdom come. Your will be done on earth as it is in heaven. Give us this day our daily bread. And forgive us our debts, as we forgive our debtors. And do not lead us into temptation, but deliver us from the evil one. For Yours is the kingdom, and the power, and the glory, forever. Amen.

MEMORY VERSE

"That you may have a walk worthy of the Lord, fully pleasing Him, being fruitful in every good work, and increasing in the knowledge of God" (Colossians 1:10).

EVENING PRAYER

LORD, God Almighty, shaper of all events, and Lord over all Your creatures, who are great in power, infinite in wisdom, and complete in justice, goodness, and mercy; we, Your creatures, made by Your hand, and upheld by Your continual power, kneel down in humble adoration of Your divine majesty. We implore You to have compassion upon us, pardoning our sins and receiving us into Your favor, for the sake of Jesus Christ, our Lord.

We desire now to confess the sins of another day; and we pray that we may do it with humble, broken, and contrite hearts. O Lord, we acknowledge our guilt in every neglect of the duties of the day, in every wrong attitude which we have indulged, and in every sinful thought and imagination. We lament our forgetfulness that we are Your creatures, accountable to You for all we do; seen by Your all-piercing eye, wherever we are. We know also we are bound, by the strongest obligations, to pay to You constant gratitude and love, to fulfill Your will, and to do all to Your glory.

We thank You for Your patience and long forbearance with us. Though we continually offend You, You still wait to be gracious; and though we have been so deaf to the calls of Your providence, and to the invitations of Your gospel, still You have not cast us off. Instead You permit us, day after day, to read Your sacred Word, to join in social prayer, and to call upon the God of our salvation.

We now ask You, for Christ's sake, to have mercy upon us. Fill our hearts with a sense of Your goodness and teach us how to serve You from now on in a more acceptable manner. Thus we may dwell in the light of Your countenance, and Your blessings may descend upon us.

Help us to be faithful in all the duties of life to which You have called us. As masters, may we remember that we have a master in heaven. As servants, may we serve the Lord Christ. As parents, may we be careful to train up our children in the nurture and admonition of the Lord. As children, may we be obedient to our parents in all things, proving that this is good and acceptable to the Lord. As citizens, may we obey civil laws and all who are put in authority over us. And, as members of the same family, may we remember how blessed a thing it is for brethren to dwell together in unity. May we, therefore, exercise toward each other all patience and charity, and may we preserve the unity of the spirit, in the bond of peace and in righteousness of life.

O Lord, pardon the sins and negligences of this day, and help us to change our ways and to live out the doctrine of God our Savior in all things.

Let us now lie down in Your favor; and, in the morning, let us again seek Your favor. And let us ever remember that You, Lord, are with us by night and by day, and that You alone cause us to dwell in safety.

These prayers we humbly present to Your divine majesty, trusting in the name of Jesus Christ our Savior. Amen.

THE grace of the Lord Jesus Christ, and the love of God, and the communion of the Holy Spirit be with you all. Amen.

MORNING PRAYER

LORD, God Almighty, whose creatures we are, to whom our prayers are constantly addressed, and whom we daily profess to serve, make available Your grace, that we may offer up to You our hearts, and place our delight in the acts of obedience to You. We ask You to strengthen our faith and to inspire our hearts with Your continual love, so that we may be enabled to triumph over those temptations to which we are exposed. Give us Your Holy Spirit; turn us from the love of sin, if we are in any way inclining to it. Put into us such an ardent desire to please You that we may be always using our time and talents in Your service. We desire to acknowledge Your right over us; we are bound to honor You by all we do.

We thank You, O Lord, that besides our obligations as creatures to the great author of our existence, You have added the most loving motives to win us to obedience. We are not our own; we are bought with a price. Your Son has died to save us. He has suffered on the cross that we might be free. He has given His life a ransom for us that He might draw us by the greatness of His love to yield our powers to Him. Therefore, being daily mindful of what our Savior has done for us, may we show that we are aware of our obligations, by the regular readiness of our minds to do and suffer all things which You shall appoint for us, or in any way require of us.

Enable us, O Lord, this day to deny ourselves, that we may live unto You. As the redeemed of the Lord, may we abstain from sin, and flee from every snare. May we be holy in all manner of conversation, respectfully impressed with a sense of Your holiness, knowing that we are called to become pure in heart, if we hope to see God. And help us to contend with the iniquity of the world around us. Let us not yield to its influence and example; but let us see ourselves as passing on to a better country, making it our great concern to escape from the snares that now surround us. May we make sure, each of us, of our own salvation and do good with the talents committed to us. Thus may we pass the day now before us; and, when the hour of our death shall come, may we then have abundant proof that we have walked by faith and not by sight, and that we shall be numbered with Your chosen people in glory everlasting.

We present these our imperfect supplications, in the name of Jesus Christ our Savior. Amen.

OUR FATHER in heaven, hallowed be Your name. Your kingdom come. Your will be done on earth as it is in heaven. Give us this day our daily bread. And forgive us our debts, as we forgive our debtors. And do not lead us into temptation, but deliver us from the evil one. For Yours is the kingdom, and the power, and the glory, forever. Amen.

MEMORY VERSE

"Blessed are the pure in heart, for they shall see God" (Matthew 5:8).

EVENING PRAYER

LMIGHTY GOD, creator of all things, in whose hands are life and death, glory be to You for all Your mercies. We thank You for Your preservation of us during the past day and for the many blessings of Your providence. Pardon, most merciful God, all the offenses against You that we have committed and also our negligence of those duties that You have required. Have mercy on our souls for Jesus Christ's sake, and give to us the comforts of Your Holy Spirit.

Enable us, O Lord, to pass our future time on earth in Your fear and to Your glory. Save us from the power of our sins and from all our spiritual enemies. You, in whose hand are the wills and affections of men, kindle in us, we ask You, all holy desires. Repress our sinful and corrupt imaginations. Dispose us to love Your commandments and to desire Your promises; strengthen and establish us in every good work; and grant that, by Your constant help and protection, we may so pass through things temporal, as finally not to lose the things eternal.

Grant, amidst the hopes and fears, the pleasures and sorrows, the dangers and deliverances—indeed, all the changes—of this mortal life, that our hearts may be surely fixed on eternal joys. O merciful Father, continually direct and bless us. Give us in this world knowledge of Your truth and confidence in Your mercy and, in the world to come, life everlasting, for the sake of Jesus Christ.

We pray, O Lord, for all our dear friends and relations. Guard them from evil by night and by day. Support, comfort, and assist them; and bring them to eternal happiness, through the merits of the same blessed Savior. Have mercy on the young. May they be trained up in the nurture and admonition of the Lord and thus learn to do Your will and to walk in Your fear, all the days of their lives.

We commend to You the president of these United States and all who are in authority. Bless all the ministers of Your gospel. Pity the sorrows of the afflicted and supply the various wants of all Your creatures. Be gracious to our benefactors. We ask You, also, to forgive our enemies and to teach us to exercise kindness and goodwill toward all men.

Take us, now, O Lord, under Your gracious protection; defend us from all the dangers of this night. Prepare us by the refreshment of sleep for the duties that

Your providence shall, on the ensuing day, appoint for us.

Accept, O Lord, these our humble and imperfect supplications, for the sake of Jesus Christ our Savior. Amen.

THE grace of the Lord Jesus Christ, and the love of God, and the communion of the Holy Spirit be with you all. Amen.

MORNING PRAYER

LMIGHTY AND EVERLASTING GOD, we acknowledge ourselves bound by innumerable obligations to praise and adore, to love and serve You. From You we have received our being. You are our constant preserver and bountiful benefactor, the source of every present enjoyment and of all hopes. You have, in Your infinite forbearance, been pleased to look down with pity on our fallen race and freely to offer salvation to us through Jesus Christ.

We adore You for the promises of Your mercy and grace, and for the joyful prospect of eternal life, so clearly revealed in Your holy Word. Impress our minds, O Lord, with that deep sense of the important truths made known to us, which shall regulate all our thoughts, words, and actions.

But while we celebrate Your goodness to us, we have cause to be ashamed of our conduct. We have great reason, O Lord, to be humbled before You, on account of the coldness and ignorance of our hearts, the disorder and lack of commitment in our loves, and the prevalence of worldly affections within us. Too often have we indulged the tempers that we ought to have subdued, and have left our duty unperformed. O Lord, be merciful to us for Your Son Jesus Christ's sake. Produce in us deep repentance and a lively faith in that Savior who has died for our sins, and has risen again for our justification.

And may Your pardoning mercy accompany the sanctifying influence of Your Spirit, that we may no more sin against You, but may live from here on as becomes the redeemed of the Lord and those qualified for a blissful immortality. Put Your fear into our hearts, that we may never more depart from You. Fix our affections on those things that are eternal. Convince us more effectively of the vanity of this world and its insufficiency to make us happy; of the evil of sin and its tendency to make us miserable; of the value of our souls and the terrors of that everlasting state, on the borders of which we stand.

We also desire to thank You for the watchful care of Your providence during the past night. We have lain down to sleep; and, blessed be Your name, we have arisen in safety. May the lives that You have prolonged be devoted to Your service. O Lord, continue to give us Your favor and protection on this day. Save us from sin and from all evil. Enable us faithfully to perform every relative duty. May we as a family dwell together in peace. May we subdue every angry passion; and, loving You with a supreme affection, may we love each other with pure hearts, fervently.

Preserve us from those temptations to which we are daily exposed. Make us aware of our weakness, so that our hearts may be often raised to You, in humble and fervent supplications for Your grace. When we are in company may it be our desire to do and to receive good. When we are alone, may we remember that our heavenly Father is with us.

Bless the president of the United States and all who are in authority. Be favorable to this nation. Visit all mankind with the light of Your gospel and let its influence increase in this land.

In tender mercy, regard all who are in affliction. Grant to our dear friends and relations every blessing that is needful for them. May they and we experience Your favor in this life, and in the world to come, life everlasting.

We offer up these our imperfect prayers in the name of Jesus Christ our Lord. Amen.

O UR FATHER *in heaven, hallowed be Your name. Your kingdom come. Your will be done on earth as it is in heaven. Give us this day our daily bread. And forgive us our debts, as we forgive our debtors. And do not lead us into temptation, but deliver us from the evil one. For Yours is the kingdom, and the power, and the glory, forever. Amen.*

MEMORY VERSE

"[He] was delivered up for our offenses, and was raised [for] our justification" (Romans 4:25).

EVENING PRAYER

O LORD GOD, our heavenly Father, who are our daily protector in all dangers and the giver of every blessing that we enjoy, we most humbly and heartily thank You for Your mercies to this family during the day that is now past. We ask You to preserve us through the night and to cause Your peace, at this time, to rest upon us.

Forgive, we ask You, all our sins. Remember not against us the transgressions of this day or of our former lives, but grant unto us true repentance and faith in our Lord Jesus Christ.

Help us daily to exercise godly sorrow for all that we do wrong. Put into us a due sense of our great unworthiness and of our continual guilt, and give to us the light of your reconciliation and the comforts of Your Holy Spirit. Thus as we lie down to rest, we shall enjoy peace in our consciences and the hope of pardon for all our sins, through Him who has died for us.

And teach us, O Lord, to number our days and to consider our latter end. Let us remember that we are continually drawing nearer to the grave and that we know not how soon it may please You to call us there. Help us to redeem the time and to fulfill the work appointed for us before we give our account to You. Let us not neglect, nor delay, to execute any good resolution that, by Your grace, we may have formed.

And, especially, may none of us delay our repentance or refuse to hear Your voice in Your gospel, lest death should come upon us unawares. Dispose us, every evening, to try and examine our ways by the standard of Your holy Word. Save us from a hardened heart, an unawakened conscience, and from a worldly and unbelieving spirit. May we remember that as Your mercies are sure to the humble and penitent, so also are Your judgments sure to him who lives and dies in his iniquity. May we, therefore, daily call upon You and truly humble ourselves before You; and may we so worship You and serve You in this world, that we may be accepted in the world to come, through the single merits of Jesus Christ our Savior.

Bless, we ask You, all our relations and friends. Make them partakers of Your grace, and of all the promises of Your gospel. Have mercy on our native land, and continue, if it please You, the blessings which we have so long and so unthankfully enjoyed. Dispose us to employ them to Your glory. Direct, we ask You, the president of the United States and all others in authority, that they may, above all things, seek Your honor. And enlighten us, O God, to discharge the Christian duties of the stations in which You have placed us.

These and all other things needful for our bodies and our souls, for our temporal and our eternal interests, we humbly ask in the name of our only mediator and intercessor Jesus Christ. Amen.

THE grace of the Lord Jesus Christ, and the love of God, and the communion of the Holy Spirit be with you all. Amen.

DAY 22

MORNING PRAYER

O LORD GOD, our heavenly Father, to whom all hearts are open and from whom no secrets are hid, we ask You to look down on us Your servants, who desire now, with true humility of soul, to offer up to You our prayers and supplications. We thank You for Your merciful protection during the past night, and we adore that goodness that has so far supplied our wants and lightened our troubles. Your goodness has preserved our lives in the midst of dangers and has caused us to lie down and rise up in peace and safety.

Now we ask You to preserve us this day from evil. Save us from all things that afflict the body, and especially from whatsoever can hurt the soul. May we go forth in Your strength to contend against the world, the flesh, and the devil; and to fulfill the various duties of our Christian calling. Save us from the sins that most easily beset us. Preserve us from idleness and negligence, as well as from presumptuous transgressions; and deliver us from that dullness of conscience which might lead us to justify ourselves though living a careless and unprofitable life. Grant to us such knowledge of You that we may love You above all things and earnestly desire to obey every precept of Your holy Word. Teach us to redeem the time, to be watchful and alert, and to abstain from all appearance of evil. Teach us to be fervent in spirit, serving the Lord, and to be never weary of well-doing; and let us take continual care, unless, through some liberty in which we indulge ourselves, we should draw others into sin, or should cause the gospel that we profess to be evil spoken of.

O Lord, help us also seriously to consider the shortness of life and the nearness of death and of eternity, that whatever our hands find to do, we may do it with all our might. Let us have our loins girded and our lamps burning, and be as servants waiting for their Lord. Let us not say in our hearts that our Lord delays His coming, but let us remember that the day of our death may overtake us suddenly, and that blessed is that servant whom His Lord when He comes shall find watching.

And grant, O most merciful God, that when finally we shall be called before Your majestic throne, to give account to Him who is the judge of the living and dead, we may hear that joyful sentence proclaimed in our ears: "Come, You blessed of my Father, inherit the kingdom prepared for you from the foundation of the world." May our portion then be with the children of God, and our inheritance among the saints.

We ask you to bless all our friends and relations. Pardon their sins, supply their temporal as well as spiritual wants, and conduct them safely, through all the temptations and dangers of this evil world, to the same land of everlasting rest and peace.

Have mercy on all for whom we are bound to pray. Aid the tempted, comfort the dejected, sustain those who are bowed down with age or with infirmity, and are drawing near to death. Have pity on all your afflicted servants, and enable them to believe that whom the Lord loves, He chastens; and that, through much tribulation, they shall enter into the Kingdom of God. And give to each of us grace to feel compassion for the various wants of others, and to minister liberally to their relief.

We offer up these our humble and imperfect prayers, in the name of our only Savior, Jesus Christ. Amen.

OUR FATHER in heaven, hallowed be Your name. Your kingdom come. Your will be done on earth as it is in heaven. Give us this day our daily bread. And forgive us our debts, as we forgive our debtors. And do not lead us into temptation, but deliver us from the evil one. For Yours is the kingdom, and the power, and the glory, forever. Amen.

MEMORY VERSE

"Redeeming the times, because the days are evil" (Ephesians 5:16).

EVENING PRAYER

LORD, our heavenly Father, we ask You to hear the prayers that we are about to offer up to You. Deliver us from all wandering thoughts; and help us to remember that we are now in the presence of that God unto whom all hearts are open, and from whom no secrets are hid.

O God, we implore You to forgive the sins of the past day. We acknowledge that we have, this day, left undone many things that we ought to have done, and done many things that we ought not to have done. We have trespassed against You in thought, word, and deed. And though we have been encouraged by Your gospel to repent of our iniquities, and to serve You in newness of life, yet we have many times returned to those sins, of which we profess to have repented; and we have fallen under Your just wrath and displeasure.

But we approach You, the God of all grace and goodness, for the sake of Your Son, Jesus Christ, to pardon all that is past. We ask You to take us into Your favor, not weighing our merits but forgiving our offenses, and causing us to place our humble trust in Your mercy. Deliver us, we ask You, from the troubles of a guilty conscience, now that we are about to lie down to rest. Save us, O Lord, from the dread of death, and from the terrors of the wrath to come. Grant to us, if it please You, a quiet night; and make us all to be at peace with You, through our Lord Jesus Christ.

At the same time we ask You not to allow that we should deceive ourselves by any false hope. Rather give us grace, day by day, to examine ourselves with care and diligence, that we may discover all that is sinful in us. O Lord, deliver us from continuing in any known sin. Save us from every secret iniquity. May each of us resolve, before we go to rest this night, to forsake, by Your grace assisting us, every former transgression; and may we devote ourselves entirely to Your service.

We further ask You to bless all our relations, friends, and acquaintances; place both them and us under Your protection this night. And have mercy on all those who are in pain, sickness, or any other adversity. Lighten their troubles and support them by Your heavenly grace.

And accept our thanks for all Your goodness given to us this day. Praised be the Lord for all His mercies: for the health and strength, and food and clothing, and comforts of every kind that we have enjoyed. But, above all, we desire to bless Your name for the gift of Jesus Christ Your Son; for the instructions of Your sacred Word; and for the hope of everlasting life. O Lord, grant to us grace to receive these, and all Your blessings, with a thankful heart; and let us show forth Your praise, not with our lips only, but with our lives.

Accept, we ask You, our imperfect supplications and prayers, for the sake of Jesus Christ, our only Lord and Savior. Amen.

THE grace of the Lord Jesus Christ, and the love of God, and the communion of the Holy Spirit be with you all. Amen.

DAY 23

MORNING PRAYER

LESSED GOD, who has caused the Holy Scriptures to be written for our learning, grant to us, we ask You, such faith in the truth of Your holy Word that we may be made partakers of your everlasting promises, through Jesus Christ our Lord.

Dispose our minds to receive, with meekness, every doctrine that You have revealed, and save us from that spiritual blindness and ignorance that naturally fill our minds. Teach us to know You, our God; to adore You for your greatness; and to admire You for Your holiness.

Open our eyes, that we may perceive ourselves to be sinners in Your sight, partakers of a fallen nature as well as actual transgressors against You. Make us to feel that we stand in continual need of both Your pardoning mercy and of Your quickening grace. And while we trust in the merits of His death and in the efficacy of His intercession, let us also acknowledge Him as our Lord, whom we are bound unreservedly to obey.

Give us grace, also, to believe the fearful threatenings of Your Word. You have declared to us that the day is coming when all who are in their graves shall come forth, they who have done good to the resurrection of life, and they who have done evil to the resurrection of condemnation. Help us to preserve in our minds the remembrance of this approaching judgment, that we may not dare to sin against You but may abound in all those fruits of holiness that You will approve in the great day of Jesus Christ.

And we ask You, O Lord, to dispose our minds to receive, with the true obedience of faith, every part of Your holy Word. May it be made profitable to us for doctrine, for correction, for reproof, for instruction in righteousness, that we may be thoroughly furnished for every good work. May we be prepared by it, not only for this our daily activity of prayer and praise and thanksgiving but for all the duties of our Christian calling. May we keep continually in our minds those things that we have learned. Then, putting on the whole armor of God, may we be able to stand fast in every evil day and to overcome the world, the flesh, and the devil.

Defend us, O Lord, we most humbly ask You, from all evil. Save us from the sins that easily besiege us. Let us control our tempers and restrain our tongues. Let us add to our faith, virtue; and to virtue, knowledge; and to knowledge, temperance; and to temperance, patience; and to patience, brotherly kindness; and to brotherly kindness, love. Let us be rich in good works, to the praise and glory of Your name. And while we are receiving Your truths into honest hearts, and are attempting by Your grace assisting us, to walk according to the precepts of Your written Word; may Your providence direct our steps in life, and watch over us for good. Defend us, we ask You, to the end of our lives; and let Your good Spirit abide within us, that we may not faint in our Christian walk, nor become weary of well-doing.

We pray for Your blessing on all our friends and relations. May they walk by the light of the same blessed gospel. May both they and we possess, in this world, knowledge of Your truth; and, in the world to come, life everlasting.

We offer up these and all our supplications in the name of Jesus Christ, our only mediator and redeemer. Amen.

OUR FATHER in heaven, hallowed be Your name. Your kingdom come. Your will be done on earth as it is in heaven. Give us this day our daily bread. And forgive us our debts, as we forgive our debtors. And do not lead us into temptation, but deliver us from the evil one. For Yours is the kingdom, and the power, and the glory, forever. Amen.

MEMORY VERSE

"Giving all diligence, add to your faith virtue, to virtue knowledge, to knowledge self-control, to self-control perseverance, to perseverance godliness, to godliness brotherly kindness, and to brotherly kindness love" (2 Peter 1:5–7).

EVENING PRAYER

LORD GOD, our heavenly Father, assist us now to draw near to You with reverence; and fill us with the Holy Spirit, that we may worship You in an acceptable manner, through Jesus Christ our Lord.

O Lord God Almighty, we thank You for all Your mercies during the past day; and we are now gathered together both to praise You for Your goodness and to commit ourselves to Your protection. Preserve us from all the dangers of this night. Grant us, if it please You, such quiet and refreshing rest that we may be prepared for all those duties of life that are before us.

We also earnestly ask You to pardon the sins that we may have committed this day. Help us now to confess them before You, examining ourselves with all impartiality and seriousness. Pardon every evil temper that we have shown this day and every rash and angry word that we may have spoken. Pardon also any lack of strict integrity in our conduct. Pardon whatsoever insincerity and hypocrisy Your holy eyes may have, this day, seen in any of us. Pardon our lack of watchfulness over ourselves and our too great readiness to cast blame continually on others. Pardon all our disobedience to Your laws; pardon also our lack of submission to Your providence and lack of zeal in Your service.

For these and all other sins that we have either on this day, or at any other time, committed, we here unite in imploring mercy, through the name of our most blessed Savior. O Lord, forgive us, for Jesus Christ's sake. Do not lay any of our past sins to our charge; but blot them out from Your remembrance, for the sake of Him who has died for us. Give us penitent and contrite hearts, and let us lie down this night in Your favor.

We also implore Your blessings on all our friends and relations. Watch over them, we ask You, by Your good providence; teach them all to live in Your fear, and to hope in Your mercy. Bless the land in which we live, and especially the faithful followers of Jesus Christ. Have pity on those who are deprived of the comforts which we enjoy; and are lying down tonight in pain, sorrow, and affliction: grant them patience to endure their sufferings; and make them at last partakers of Your heavenly kingdom. And teach us, O Lord, to have compassion on the afflicted; and to pray for them; and to do good to all men; and to live in peace and harmony one with another.

We offer up these imperfect prayers in the name of Jesus Christ, our only Lord and Savior. Amen.

THE grace of the Lord Jesus Christ, and the love of God, and the communion of the Holy Spirit be with you all. Amen.

MORNING PRAYER

LORD, our heavenly Father, through whose providential goodness we are now permitted to see the light of another day, grant unto us grace to devote the lives that You lengthen to Your service.

Assist us in all the duties to which we shall be called this day, and direct us to the employment that shall best fit us. You have appointed unto every man his work in life. Help us to be faithful and diligent in our calling; to be, at the same time, cheerful and contented with our lot; and, in all our earthly activities, to be mindful of a better world. Deliver us from all those anxieties and cares by which we are overly distracted.

We desire to remember that our lives are but shadows that soon pass away; and that the difficulties and trials that we must meet with here will soon cease forever. Teach us, also, moderation in our temporal enjoyments. May we chiefly desire those spiritual blessings that bring comfort to the soul. Grant unto us pardon of our sins and a true faith in Jesus Christ, our Lord. Enable us to lay hold of the promises of Your gospel, and to delight ourselves with the sense of Your favor here, and with the hope of eternal life hereafter. And make all things to work together for our good. Be pleased to so order the events of our lives that we may see continual reason to praise You for Your blessings toward us. Thus, being guided by Your providence and sanctified by Your Spirit, may we attain finally to the end of our faith—the salvation of our souls.

We pray, also, for all our dear friends and relations. Pardon, O Lord, their trespasses and sins, and make them partakers of the promises of Christ in His gospel. Lead them through their various temptations and trials; make them happy in themselves and blessings to us and to all around them.

Have pity on the sons and daughters of affliction: sanctify to them their troubles in this life, and teach them to rejoice in the Lord amidst all their worldly tribulation. Bless the rising generation, and may there be never wanting in this land a seed to serve You.

We pray, especially, that the children of this family may be brought up in Your fear. May the Lord save them from this evil world. May the Lord strengthen, establish, and settle them; and, after a life full of good works, give them an abundant entrance into His heavenly kingdom.

We present these our imperfect prayers in the name of Jesus Christ, our ever-blessed redeemer. Amen.

OUR FATHER *in heaven, hallowed be Your name. Your kingdom come. Your will be done on earth as it is in heaven. Give us this day our daily bread. And forgive us our debts, as we forgive our debtors. And do not lead us into temptation, but deliver us from the evil one. For Yours is the kingdom, and the power, and the glory, forever. Amen.*

MEMORY VERSE

"And we know that all things work together for good to those who love God, and who are the called according to His purpose" (Romans 8:28).

EVENING PRAYER

LMIGHTY AND EVERLASTING GOD, we bless You for Your great goodness in creating, preserving, and redeeming us, and for all Your various mercies from our birth unto this hour. We adore You as the author of all things, but especially as our Father and our friend, the God of our lives. You are the source of our hopes and the giver of all spiritual as well as temporal good.

We desire to praise You for the gift of Jesus Christ, Your Son, by whom we obtain pardon of sin, and all things necessary for our eternal salvation. We thank You that He descended into our world and has set us an example by His holy life. By His resurrection from the grave on the third day He has also given assurance that He is able to raise our bodies from the dust and to exalt us to His own right hand in the kingdom of Heaven.

We ask You, O Lord, to impress deeply on our minds these great and solemn truths, that we may not forget them amidst the cares and occupations of the world. May we be reminded daily of our Christian privileges, as well as of the duties to which we are called. Convince us of the vanity of the world, of the shortness of life, and of the unspeakable importance of eternity. Save us from indifference, thoughtlessness, and levity, as well as from wickedness and sin. Purify our hearts by Your Holy Spirit, and teach us habitually to remember that You see our secret thoughts and require truth in the inward parts.

Pardon, we ask You, the multitude of our sins in times past: our pride and vanity, our covetousness and worldliness, our anger and passion, our laziness and negligence, our too careless performance of the duties of our station, and our lack of Christian kindness and of brotherly love. Pardon, especially, our forgetfulness of You, our God. How seldom have we thought of You; how coldly have we worshiped You; how little have we honored You as we ought! You have caused us to abound with the good things of this life—Your hand has protected us; Your goodness has raised us, when, through sickness, or calamity, we have been brought low—so that we are under peculiar obligations to love and serve You, and to praise and magnify Your holy name. O Lord, forgive our ingratitude to You our great benefactor; and enable us to trust in Jesus Christ, for the remission of every sin, as well as for the acceptance of those imperfect services that we would offer up to You.

We implore You to send Your blessed gospel over the world. May the nations hear the joyful sound; may Your kingdom come and Your will be done on earth as it is in heaven. Bless the labors of Your ministers in every place. Fill them with zeal of Your honor, and with love to Your name. May multitudes in this land repent and believe, and may the spirit of true religion both revive among ourselves and spread over all nations. May Christ be preached from the rising to the setting sun, and may each of us try to recommend those truths that we have been taught, that there may be no occasion for the enemies of the gospel to blaspheme us.

We would intercede for all our relations, acquaintances and friends, especially for those who are in sorrow, sickness, or trouble. Grant to them those consolations that You alone can bestow. Put into their hearts a holy trust in You, and a sure hope in Your promises. And may those who feel that their infirmities come upon them and that their outward frame decays be enabled to believe that, when earthly things fail, they shall have a lasting building from God. Not a house made with hands, but one that is eternal in the heavens.

Take us now, O God, under Your gracious care this night. Let Your blessing attend us and Your good Spirit rest upon us. And may we get up and lie down at peace with You and under a continual sense of Your presence.

We offer up our imperfect supplications, in the name of Jesus Christ, our Mediator and Redeemer. Amen.

THE grace of the Lord Jesus Christ, and the love of God, and the communion of the Holy Spirit be with you all. Amen.

DAY 25

MORNING PRAYER

LMIGHTY AND EVER-BLESSED GOD, You are father of all the families of the earth, and the ever-present help of those who put their trust in You. Amid the weakness of infancy You have sustained us; in youth You have guided us; and during our advancing years You have preserved us. By Your providence we are united in one household, for You have supplied our wants and abundantly provided as well for our bodies, as for our souls. You, O great God, have delivered us from some of the scenes of temptation, and of sorrow, to which we see others exposed; and now have permitted us to lie down and rise up in peace and safety. Thus we are now meeting together to thank You for the mercies of the past night, and to acknowledge that it is by Your power and goodness alone that we are preserved from day to day.

O Lord, protect us this day from evil. Go forth with us to the several duties of our callings, and enable us to do all things in honor of You, and to Your glory.

We beseech You to pour Your Spirit into our heart, that we may not depart from You nor forget any of Your commandments. May we serve You with humble, patient, and quiet minds, and may our love abound both toward You and toward all men. Deliver us from those angry tempers to which our natures are so prone, and from all those sins that war against the soul. And may we grow in grace: may we, more and more, prevail over the temptations by which we have formerly been overcome. May we lay aside every weight, and the sins that have easily beset us; ever looking to Him who is the author and finisher of our faith, and pressing toward the mark of the prize of our high calling in Christ Jesus. May we remember that, in due time, we shall reap if we do not faint, and may we be steadfast, immovable, always abounding in the work of the Lord. May we be faithful, even unto death, knowing that our labor shall not be in vain in the Lord.

We pray for Your special blessing on the employments in which we shall this day engage. May we undertake nothing that is contrary to Your will, and may our good works be crowned by You with success. We would remember that without You we can do nothing. Indeed, remind us that without the agreement of Your providence, we can fulfill no purpose of our minds, and that we can do nothing spiritually good without the aid of Your grace. Unto You, therefore, let our eyes be continually lifted up.

Bless, O Lord, every member of this family. Grant unto the children a spirit of teachableness and obedience and may none of us forget You our God, nor be indifferent to the great and glorious hope which You have set before us. O grant that in all our works—begun, continued, and ended in You—we may, each of us, glorify Your holy name.

Have mercy on all our friends and relations. Pity the poor and the afflicted. Give peace to those who are troubled in mind, and supply the various necessities of all Your creatures.

We ask every blessing, in the name of Jesus Christ. Amen.

O*UR FATHER in heaven, hallowed be Your name. Your kingdom come. Your will be done on earth as it is in heaven. Give us this day our daily bread. And forgive us our debts, as we forgive our debtors. And do not lead us into temptation, but deliver us from the evil one. For Yours is the kingdom, and the power, and the glory, forever. Amen.*

MEMORY VERSE

"Looking unto Jesus, the author and finisher of our faith, who for the joy that was set before Him endured the cross, despising the shame, and has sat down at the right hand of the throne of God" (Hebrews 12:2).

EVENING PRAYER

LMIGHTY AND EVERLASTING GOD, our creator, preserver, and redeemer, we now enter into Your sacred presence, under a deep sense of our weakness and unworthiness, and of Your unspeakable greatness and majesty. We approach You, at the same time, as a God of goodness and mercy; for You have made Yourself known to us in Jesus Christ Your Son and have proclaimed pardon to every repenting sinner through faith in that sacrifice which He has offered on the cross, for us. We desire to bless You for this strong foundation of our hope, and we would now address You in the full assurance of faith, renouncing all confidence in ourselves, rejoicing in Him who has become the hope of all the ends of the earth, and is the Lamb slain from the foundation of the world. We praise the Lamb who died for us, has risen again, and is now exalted at Your right hand, where He ever lives to make intercession for us.

We beseech You, O God, to accept for His sake our imperfect worship that we offer up to You. Having been taught to know Your will, may we be diligent to fulfill it. You have given us line upon line, and precept upon precept, and have placed us in the midst of light and knowledge. Grant unto us a true and lively faith in all the doctrines of Your holy Word, and a spirit of unreserved obedience to them.

We ask You to make us diligent and faithful in all the occupations of life to which in Your providence we shall be called. Let us not live in indolence and self-indulgence, but let us attempt to be useful in our generation. Let us be fervent in spirit, serving the Lord. Let us walk in Your fear from day to day, and in all things aim to please our heavenly Father. Make us to be the same in secret as we would wish to be in public.

We ask You to inspire us with a spirit of Christian kindness to all around us. You have been bountiful and gracious to us. You have multiplied our temporal comforts, and You pardon our numberless transgressions. Grant that we may follow the example of Your generosity and that we may also be like You, ready to forgive. May we be watchful over ourselves but tender toward the infirmities of others.

Strengthen us in our seasons of trial and temptation; guide us through all the difficulties into which we may fall; and bless us in all the scenes of life through which we may pass. If afflictions should come upon us, inspire us with humble resignation to Your will: You, O Lord, do not willingly grieve the children of men; do not chastise us in Your indignation; but turn the mournful events of Your providence to our spiritual and endless good.

Prepare us by all the events of life for our great and final change, for we know not how soon it may come upon us. May the occurrence of Your sabbaths and the preaching of Your word—may every opportunity of holy meditation, and of public, social, and secret prayer—call our minds from this earthly scene, that we may be fitted for that everlasting state. When the shadows of the evening shall come upon us, when age and sickness shall arrive, and human help shall fail, be, O Lord, the strength of our hearts and our portion forevermore.

Bless our president and all who are in authority; give wisdom to our houses of Congress. Save us from public war, as well as from internal discord. Bless every attempt to spread Your true gospel among the nations. Crown as well with Your continual blessing the labors of the ministers of Your gospel in our own favored country.

And, finally, we ask You to take us all under Your protection this night. Grant to our frail bodies that refreshment which is needful for them; and enable us to lie down, exercising a holy trust in You, and having fervent charity toward all men.

We offer up these our imperfect prayers in the name of our blessed Savior Jesus Christ. Amen.

THE grace of the Lord Jesus Christ, and the love of God, and the communion of the Holy Spirit be with you all. Amen.

MORNING PRAYER

LMIGHTY AND MOST MERCIFUL GOD, we ask You to pour down Your blessing on us Your servants, who are now assembled to worship Your holy name.

You are infinitely great and glorious! Before You the angels veil their faces, and the heavens are not pure in Your sight. We are weak and helpless, sinful, and corrupt, exposed to dangers on every side and in continual need of Your gracious assistance. O Lord, preserve us through this day. Guard, we ask You, both our bodies and our souls from every kind of evil.

We are now beginning the duties of our various callings. Enable each of us to be faithful and diligent in them, as those who must hereafter give an account of all things done in the body, to Him who is the Judge of the living and dead.

We pray that all our most secret ways may be pleasing to You, O searcher of hearts. Let us not attempt to deceive either ourselves or those around us by the mere appearance of goodness, but may we have the witness of our consciences, that in simplicity and godly sincerity we have our dealings with the world.

Give us grace to overcome our sinful appetites and passions, to mortify our pride, and to bring every member of our bodies and ever faculty of our souls into captivity to the law of Christ. May we put away all hatred and division, all anger and strife, all malice and evil speaking; and may this day be a day of peace and harmony for every member of this family.

We ask You to bless the events that shall come to us on this day. You, O Lord, order all things for us, and we do not know what a day may bring forth. Sanctify to us our prosperity and our adversity, our health and our sickness, our daily comforts and enjoyments, as well as our anxieties and disappointments.

We desire, also, to give You our grateful thanks for Your past mercies. You have sustained us in our infancy, guided us in youth, and preserved us during our advancing years. You have often raised us when we have been brought low: You have comforted us in trouble and have delivered us in sickness. While others have fallen, we have been kept alive. Day after day we remain the models of Your mercy, and comforts surround us on every side. O Lord, we bless Your name for what is past, and we pray that the remembrance of Your goodness may lead us to repentance and may make us careful to walk according to Your will, for the days that are yet to come.

We further ask You to bestow Your blessing on our dear friends and relations. You have encouraged and commanded us to intercede for one another; and we desire, therefore, most earnestly to commend to Your fatherly care all those whom it is our duty to remember in our prayers. We ask You to be merciful to those who have at any time shown us mercy, to pity the poor and the afflicted, to strengthen the weak, and to comfort the despondent mind.

Have mercy on the rising generation. Save them from the follies and ignorances of their youth, and raise them up to be a seed to serve You, when we shall be gathered to our fathers in death.

Hear us, O Lord, in these our prayers and intercessions, for the sake of our only Savior, Jesus Christ. Amen.

O UR FATHER in heaven, hallowed be Your name. Your kingdom come. Your will be done on earth as it is in heaven. Give us this day our daily bread. And forgive us our debts, as we forgive our debtors. And do not lead us into temptation, but deliver us from the evil one. For Yours is the kingdom, and the power, and the glory, forever. Amen.

MEMORY VERSE

"We conducted ourselves in the world in simplicity and godly sincerity, not with fleshly wisdom, but by the grace of God" (2 Corinthians 1:12).

EVENING PRAYER

LORD, God Almighty, who understands the secrets of every heart and is also a God of infinite perfection and purity, we sinners, who in thought, word, and deed, have offended against You, desire most humbly to confess our sins and to implore Your merciful forgiveness.

We ask You to assist us by Your Holy Spirit to know wherein we have sinned against You. You who claim not only the outward service of Your creatures, but require truth in the inward parts, give us a deep conviction of the necessity of seriously examining ourselves. May we compare all our ways with the standard of Your holy law, that we may thus become aware of our transgressions, and, freely confessing them before that God whom we have offended, may obtain perfect forgiveness through our Lord and Savior Jesus Christ.

O Lord, we acknowledge our forgetfulness of You and the rebellion of our hearts against You. We have not honored You as God, but have set up our own will as our law, choosing to follow our own vain imaginations. We have neglected Your written word; we have not duly attended to the instructions of Your ministers; we have been careless even with the means of grace; and not very willing to use the sabbath for our spiritual edification.

You have called to us by many dispensations of Your providence, often reminding us of our latter end. You have shown us the vanity of all our earthly hopes and have taught us lessons of wisdom, both by the afflictions and by the various trials and disappointments with which You have visited us. But we have too often complained at Your providence, instead of profiting by it, and have objected to our condition in life instead of turning our thoughts to a happier and better world.

Or if You have multiplied our comforts, how prone we have been to place our chief happiness in these, and not in You, who are the Giver. How many and various have been our sins, both secret and open, from our youth until this time! How many have been the sinful thoughts that we have indulged; of which You, and You only, have been the witness. For such thoughts, unless they are repented of in this world, You will call us to account in the day of judgment. How many rash and angry words, also, have we continually spoken. How often have we injured our neighbors, judging others harshly, while we hope to be judged mercifully by You. Not willing to forgive, nonetheless we ourselves hope to be forgiven.

We would confess, O Lord, the ungodliness of our hearts and lives, and the frequent impatience of our spirits. You have appointed our lot in life, and have ordered all things concerning us, but how little have we carried out the stations in which You have placed us. How unfaithfully have we employed the talents entrusted to us; and how soon have we been weary in well-doing!

We request of You to make us duly aware of all the sins, whereby we have offended against You. Give us grace to repent and turn to You, to believe in the name of our Lord Jesus Christ, and to walk in newness of life. We thank You that there is forgiveness preached to us in our Savior's name; that we are encouraged to confess our sins, renew our repentance, and to call upon the Lord our God. And, O Lord, grant unto us, together with the pardon of our sins the aid of Your Spirit, that whatever truths we have heard this day may make a serious and lasting impression, and that whatever sins have been this day brought to our remembrance may be repented of and forsaken.

May we be enabled especially to contend against those sins that have easily beset us. O Lord, bless us in the ensuing week. May it be spent in a manner worthy of our Christian profession, and of our supplications unto You. Be our counselor and guide, and our defender in whom we trust. Guard us from all dangers and continually keep us in all our ways. We ask You to maintain Your grace in us, and bring us finally to Your everlasting kingdom, through our Lord and Savior Jesus Christ. Amen.

THE grace of the Lord Jesus Christ, and the love of God, and the communion of the Holy Spirit be with you all. Amen.

MORNING PRAYER

LMIGHTY AND EVERLASTING GOD, who are the author of our being, the preserver of our lives, and the giver of every blessing that we enjoy, unto You do we now direct our prayer, asking You this day to supply our wants and necessities. Grant unto us all things needful both for the body and soul, and especially give to us pardon of our sins, through Jesus Christ our Lord.

We confess that we are unworthy of Your favor, for we have continually trespassed against You; but You are good, and gracious to those who freely acknowledge their transgressions and cast themselves on Your mercy. O Lord, we pray that we, being delivered from the fear of Your wrath through a lively faith in Jesus Christ Your Son, may serve You with cheerful and quiet minds. We desire to partake in all the consolations of Your Spirit as well as walk in the way of Your commandments.

We pray for integrity and diligence in our various

callings. May we remember today that Your eye is upon us. May we carefully avoid hypocrisy and deceit and every hint of dishonesty and unfaithfulness. May we, also, guard against pride and vanity, against envy and hatred, against selfishness and covetousness, and against whatever sin may most easily beset us. May we each fulfill our proper work with humility of mind and serve not only those around us but You also, God, who searches the heart.

May we, likewise, exercise fervent love toward all men. Teach us to weep with those who weep, and to rejoice with those who rejoice, and to minister to the utmost of our fellow creatures. In this way may we follow the example of our Lord and Savior, who has taught us that it is more blessed to give than to receive. And grant to us grace in every respect to display by our lives the holy gospel that we profess.

We ask You, also, to guide our future steps. Be our constant helper and defender, ordaining for us that condition in life that shall be most conducive to our eternal welfare. If You send trouble, impart to us strength to bear it, and save us from those temptations that might provide the occasion for our falling. If prosperity be our lot, give us grace to be thankful for it and to use with moderation our many enjoyments. May we remember that the time is short—that our light affliction is but for a moment, that our earthly pleasures also will soon be past, that all the glory of man is but as the flower of the grass, and that the ways of this world pass away.

We would, furthermore, intercede with You on behalf of all our friends and relations. Bless them in their personal lives, in their families, and in all their under-takings. Grant them the comforts of Your grace here, and make them finally partakers of glory everlasting.

We implore You to bestow special favor on the rising generation. Save them from the corruption of this vain and evil world. Watch over them during the weakness and inexperience of their youth and prepare them for the duties to which Your providence shall call them.

We give over to Your fatherly care the poor and desti-tute, the prisoner, the sick, and the afflicted. Send help from above to those who are under severe temptations: strengthen the feeble knees, and raise up those who have fallen. Teach us all to exercise patience and for-bearance and kindness toward each other.

We offer these our imperfect prayers, in the name of our only Savior, Jesus Christ. Amen.

*O*UR FATHER *in heaven, hallowed be Your name. Your kingdom come. Your will be done on earth as it is in heaven. Give us this day our daily bread. And forgive us our debts, as we forgive our debtors. And do not lead us into temptation, but deliver us from the evil one. For Yours is the kingdom, and the power, and the glory, forever. Amen.*

MEMORY VERSE

"For our light affliction, which is but for a moment, is working for us a far more exceeding and eternal weight of glory" (2 Corinthians 4:17).

EVENING PRAYER

LORD, our heavenly Father, we ask You to accept the worship that we have given to You on this Your day. Give Your abundant blessing to all the means of grace and impart to us a full conviction of those doctrines of Your gospel that have been delivered to us. May they not only arouse our fears and hopes, but may they be engraved on all our hearts, by the power of Your Holy Spirit.

You have favored us with many and great advantages. You have enlightened us by Your holy Word. You have sent us ministers instructed in Your truths, and have multiplied our opportunities of edification. You have removed from us many obstacles that others meet with in their heavenly course, and You have made our way clear.

We bless You, O Lord, for these unspeakable mercies; but we would rejoice with trembling, knowing that to whom much is given, of them shall much be required. O

Lord, grant unto us Your Holy Spirit; to enlighten our darkness, to strengthen our weakness, and to supply all that is wanting in us for our spiritual needs, and for the everlasting salvation of our souls.

We ask You to reveal in our hearts the abounding grace and love of Christ, that we may be delivered from the fears that bind us and may advance with cheerful and willing steps in the way of Your commandments. Give us that hope, which is the anchor of the soul, sure and steadfast. Bless us with that most excellent gift of love, without which we are as sounding brass, and tinkling cymbal. May we more plainly perceive, and more often reflect on, the cause of our having so imperfectly obeyed You in times past. O God, we have not loved You and, therefore, we have not served You as we ought. Our hearts have been too cold and lifeless. Christ our Savior has died for us, but we have remained little affected by all that He did and suffered for us.

Do impress upon us those all-powerful doctrines of Your Word that are able to draw our hearts to You, and especially may redeeming love, that great theme of the gospel, be the favorite subject of our meditation. And grant, O Lord, that, having learned to love You for Your unspeakable mercies in Jesus Christ, and having obtained an interest in His salvation, we may have the consolation of trusting that we are safe in life, in death, and in eternity. May we pass through all the future scenes of life secure from the sins by which we have been overcome; and having overcome some of the trials that once threatened us, may the recollection be an encouragement for us to trust, that we shall, in due time, triumph over them all.

Give us such a deep sense of our obligations to our blessed Savior, and such a steadfast hope of immortal life through Him, that no temptations may prevail over us. May we be occupied whenever we may have periods of rest by the hope of heaven and the love of Christ; and when we are engaged in business in the world, may our love for You inspire us with such continual zeal in doing good, and such holy activity in our calling, that we may be preserved from those snares to which the careless and the profane are constantly exposed. And thus may we pass on through life, growing in grace, attached more and more to every principle of the gospel, looking to the author and finisher of our faith, and anticipating a happy resurrection. May we hold fast the profession of our faith without wavering. May we obtain from You, by daily prayer, the constant aid of Your heavenly grace; we ask it for Jesus Christ our Savior's sake. Amen.

THE grace of the Lord Jesus Christ, and the love of God, and the communion of the Holy Spirit be with you all. Amen.

DAY 28

MORNING PRAYER

LORD GOD, our heavenly Father, who are the giver of all good things, we desire to thank You for Your mercies during the past night, and for all the numberless blessings we enjoy. We would begin this day with Your solemn worship, thus acknowledging Your hand in the fullness of Your providence, and expressing our gratitude and obedience to You. We would, also, praise You for the gift of Jesus Christ Your Son, by whom we obtain pardon for sin, and all things necessary for our everlasting salvation. We adore Your name that you have not left us in ignorance of You but have given us Your holy Word; You have caused us to be rich with the means of grace. We would daily remember Your spiritual gifts, and we would now resolve to spend this day in a manner worthy of our Christian profession.

Assist us, O Lord, by Your Holy Spirit, to bring our prayers to fruition. Strengthen us against our tempta-

175

tions. Direct us in every difficulty, comfort us in all our sorrows and adversities, and enable us to fulfill every part of our Christian duty in which we have been instructed.

May we love our neighbor as ourselves; and do unto all men as we would that they should do to us. May we honor and obey the civil authority. May we submit ourselves to all our governors and teachers. May we hurt no one by word or deed. May we be true and just in all our dealings, and bear no ill will nor hatred in our hearts. May we keep our hands from stealing and our tongues from evil speaking, lying, and slander. May we preserve our bodies in temperance, soberness, and chastity. And may we not covet other men's goods, but learn and labor truly to earn our living and to do our duty in that state of life to which You have called us.

Pardon all our negligence in time past; and give us grace continually to examine ourselves and to conform our lives according to Your holy Word.

We desire to add our humble supplications for all those whom it is our duty to remember in our prayers. Have compassion on the poor and the afflicted. Send them help, O Lord, in their hour of need; sustain them with Your heavenly blessings when all human aid shall fail. We pray for the young and the ignorant. May they be instructed in the way in which they ought to live, and may they become instruments to extend the knowledge of You and of Your Son Jesus Christ to distant generations.

Hear us, O Lord, in these imperfect prayers, which we humbly present to You, in the name of our blessed Savior Jesus Christ. Amen.

OUR FATHER in heaven, hallowed be Your name. Your kingdom come. Your will be done on earth as it is in heaven. Give us this day our daily bread. And forgive us our debts, as we forgive our debtors. And do not lead us into temptation, but deliver us from the evil one. For Yours is the kingdom, and the power, and the glory, forever. Amen.

MEMORY VERSE

"You shall love your neighbor as yourself" (Matthew 19:19).

EVENING PRAYER

LMIGHTY AND MOST MERCIFUL GOD, who has encouraged and commanded us in Your Word both to make known our wants and to confess our sins, we desire now to approach the throne of Your grace, deeply aware of our many needs, and imploring Your forgiving mercy.

We ask You to have compassion upon us for the sake of Your Son Jesus Christ. Blessed be Your name for this great mediator between God and man through whom alone we hope for acceptance in our prayers and for all things necessary for both the body and the soul. We have sinned grievously against You; we have trespassed in thought, word, and deed. We have left undone that which we ought to have done, as well as done that which we ought not to have done, and there is no strength in us. We cannot tell how often we have offended You. O Lord, cleanse us from our secret faults.

Teach us to know ourselves, that we may more fully understand our great unworthiness and more entirely rely on Your grace in Jesus Christ.

We would especially lament the sins of the past week. We attempt, day by day, to improve our lives, but too often we leave a great part of our duty unperformed. We yield to laziness and negligence, to selfishness and covetousness, to our evil tempers, and to many sins that easily beset us; and our daily repentance is incomplete. Assist us now to acknowledge, with deep contrition of soul, the guilt that we carry, that we may obtain perfect remission of sins through the Savior in whom You have encouraged us to hope.

And grant to us, for His sake, the power of Your Holy Spirit, that we may be enabled to advance in our Christian walk and prevail over the enemies of our souls. Save us from the world, the flesh, and the devil. Give us strength, that we may fight under the banners of our Savior; and may be made more than conquerors over every temptation. May we become habitually fearful of sinning against You, and diligent in every good work.

We ask You to grant Your blessing to the Scripture we have read this day; that it may be grafted inwardly in all our hearts and may bring forth in us the fruit of good living. May our faith be strengthened by every religious exercise in which we engage, and may we be prepared for an eternal sabbath, in Your immediate presence in heaven.

Give success to every effort made on this day to bring

sinners to repentance, by missionaries abroad and evangelists at home. Let Your name be known on earth, Your saving health to all nations. May they who sit in darkness behold the Sun of Righteousness arise, and may Your Word everywhere be glorified.

We pray for all who are appointed to spread Your truth. O Lord, enlighten them by Your grace so that they may be able to instruct others, and lead them safely forward in the way of everlasting life.

Have mercy on the land in which we live. Bless our president. Inspire our judges with integrity and our people with the spirit of obedience. Have pity on the poor and the afflicted. Give your blessing to the rising generation. May they be trained up in the nurture and admonition of the Lord and advance not only in useful knowledge but in all virtue and godliness.

Finally we pray for our Christian friends and for all our dear relations. Being united in the bonds of Christian love, may we all seek each other's welfare and bear each other's burdens and thus fulfill the law of Christ. May those who are strong have grace to bear with the infirmities of the weak, and may we minister to each other's necessities according to our opportunity and ability. We present these imperfect prayers in the name of Jesus Christ our Lord and Savior. Amen.

THE grace of the Lord Jesus Christ, and the love of God, and the communion of the Holy Spirit be with you all. Amen.

DAY 29

MORNING PRAYER

LMIGHTY AND EVER-BLESSED GOD, You are the King eternal, immortal and invisible. You sit in the highest heavens and are exalted above all blessing and praise; before You the angels veil their faces, and the heavens are not pure in Your sight. You created all things, You uphold all things, You sustain the lives of the creatures whom You have made. And You govern all events by Your unceasing providence.

We bless You that, out of Your great goodness, You have sent Your Son Jesus Christ to redeem forever from death and hell our immortal souls. We bless you, too, that You have given us an assurance of our own resurrection, by raising Him from the dead on the third day.

We praise You for corporate worship, on which we maintain an ongoing remembrance of this victory of our once crucified and now ascended Lord. Grant, we ask You, that we may this day read Your sacred Word with reverence and holy fear, with serious and deep atten-

181

tion, and with all humility and thankfulness. Enable us to pray with devout and contrite hearts; and be pleased to bless our private meditations, that we may be made partakers of Your everlasting promises in Christ Jesus and may advance in all holiness.

O Lord, strengthen our faith by means of those spiritual disciplines in which we shall engage. Give us an increasing sense of our unworthiness, and a clearer knowledge of those sins that most easily beset us, that we may more fully comprehend the riches of Your grace in Christ and may, also, better know how to reform the evil within us.

Do not allow any of us to continue to be self-deceived. Let not death overtake us unprepared; instead, by Your Holy Spirit, give such power to the preaching of Your Word, and to all other means of grace, that we may heartily repent and sincerely believe and bring forth abundant fruits of true repentance, to the praise and glory of Your name.

Let Your blessing everywhere accompany the preaching of Your gospel this Sunday. May the God of grace pour forth the abundance of His Spirit on the ministers and on the hearers. May they who have lived in sin be awakened to a sense of their danger. May the unbelievers be convinced, the thoughtless be alarmed, and the weak be strengthened. May the young be guided in the right way, and the afflicted soul be comforted. May the foundation of Your universal church be enlarged, and may believers be built up in faith, hope, and love and learn to understand what is the good and acceptable and perfect will of God.

Extend Your special blessing on those who are laboring to extend in foreign lands the knowledge of a crucified Redeemer. Assist them by Your providence and grace, that they may contend successfully against idolatry and superstition. Strengthen them by Your Holy Spirit; and, in the midst of all their difficulties and trials, impart to them the fullness of Your comfort. Open the hearts of many to receive Your gospel and love it wholeheartedly. Let the light spring up to them who have long sat in darkness. And let the days come when the lion shall lie down with the lamb, when wars shall cease, and the knowledge of the Lord shall cover the earth as the waters cover the sea.

Hear us, O Lord, in these prayers and intercessions, for the sake of Jesus Christ, our only mediator and redeemer. Amen.

O*UR FATHER in heaven, hallowed be Your name. Your kingdom come. Your will be done on earth as it is in heaven. Give us this day our daily bread. And forgive us our debts, as we forgive our debtors. And do not lead us into temptation, but deliver us from the evil one. For Yours is the kingdom, and the power, and the glory, forever. Amen.*

MEMORY VERSE

"Now to the King eternal, immortal, invisible, to God who alone is wise, be honor and glory forever and ever" (1 Timothy 1:17).

EVENING PRAYER

LORD GOD, our heavenly Father, who preserves us from year to year and continually renews Your various mercies to us, we kneel down this evening, desiring to express our gratitude and love to You, who are the author of our being and the source of all our happiness.

We thank You that while so many thousands are suffering in misery and want, we are provided with innumerable comforts and are living day after day in quietness and peace.

We ask You, O Lord, that, as we look back on our days that have passed and consider our lot in life, we may become more thankful for all that goodness that is showered down upon us. In fulfilling Your will, may we become more earnest to use the opportunities and talents that are given to us. Concerning your providential gifts, we lament every neglect and abuse of which we may have been guilty of in times past; we confess with shame and humiliation of our soul that our talents have not been turned to a religious and profitable use, as they ought to have been.

We would now, especially, repent of our misspent time, neglected opportunities, and all our other sins during the past day. We have indulged in many sinful thoughts. We have uttered many hasty and unbecoming words. And how little have we attempted to exercise every Christian grace! We are sorry also, for the coldness of our hearts in our religious duties. Though instructed in the wonderful truths of the gospel, and blessed with the knowledge of Christ crucified for us, we confess that we have been listless and lukewarm in our worship, very much alienated from the life of God, and too occupied with the cares of this world. Though living, O Lord, on Your continual bounty, kept by Your power, and indebted to Your pardoning grace, how little have we labored to fulfill Your holy will, and to walk blamelessly in all Your statues and commandments.

We now present ourselves before You, freely confessing these sins and imploring Your forgiveness in the name of Jesus Christ. We lie down tonight trusting in His all-sufficient sacrifice on the cross for us and looking for Your mercy leading to eternal life.

And we pray that, being prepared by repentance and deep humiliation of soul, we may go forth on the next Sunday to hear Your gospel, with teachable and submissive minds. May we receive the seed sown into an honest and good heart. May the gospel of our salvation be the chief desire of our minds, and the consolation of all our hearts. May we bless the God, who not only increases our temporal mercies, but also sets before us the hope of everlasting life.

O Lord, enable each of us who profess the name of Christ, to set an example of pure and undefiled religion to all who live around us.

Have compassion on the young in this family. Incline them to hear Your word with attention, that they may grow wiser every day they live; and teach them to lift up their hearts in prayer, while they kneel down with us to worship You.

Confirm the wavering in the ways of true religion. May they see that godliness has the promise of the life that now is, as well as of the life that is to come. May they, also, be convinced of their sins and experience what is that peace of conscience, which the gospel brings to the truly humble and penitent.

To You we now commit ourselves, asking You to bless every member of this family. May we lie down in the fear of God, in the faith of Christ, and in the comfort of the Holy Spirit; and may we rise in the morning, rejoicing in our Christian privileges, and desiring to use the day in Your service.

Hear us, O Lord, in these supplications, for Jesus Christ's sake. Amen.

THE grace of the Lord Jesus Christ, and the love of God, and the communion of the Holy Spirit be with you all. Amen.

DAY 30

MORNING PRAYER

LMIGHTY AND EVERLASTING GOD, who did make man in Your own image; and, when he had fallen from his first estate, did send your Son from heaven to save him, we ask You to give us grace this day to study Your holy Word.

We would begin our duties humbly asking You to impress our minds to earnestly desire those things that concern our salvation. Deliver us from the love of this world and from the many anxieties and cares to which, through the sinfulness and frailty of our nature, we are continually prone. Elevate our thoughts to things above. Convince us of the shortness of time and of the value of eternity, of the uncertainty of our mortal state, and of the near approach of that day when we shall give account of all things done in the body. O Lord, what is our life? It is as a watch in the night; it is as a vapor that vanishes away; as the grass of the field, which in the evening is cut down and withers. But though we know that we must

187

shortly die and that here all is vanity and stress of spirit, we desire to bless Your holy name, that, however few and evil may be the days of our pilgrimage, You have provided us with many great and glorious hopes.

O grant us grace to lay hold on those promises that are set before us and to give all diligence, that we may make our calling and election sure. Thus may that world in which we dwell become the door of entrance to a better state, the passage to a heavenly Canaan, the blessed means of bringing us to You, our Father, and to Jesus Christ our Savior.

May we examine ourselves, repent of our sins, and renew our vows of obedience to You. May we shake off our indolence and self-indulgence and learn, more and more, to walk in the Spirit, and to mortify the whole body of sin. And while we thus strive to purify our souls through the love of the truth, may Your Word come to us with increasing power, with demonstration of the Spirit, and with much assurance. May we grow in the knowledge of You and of Your Son Jesus Christ, and may we abound more and more in faith, hope, and love.

O Lord, go forth with us this day as we worship You; and pour down upon us Your Holy Spirit. Hold back our vain, fleshly desires. Encourage our minds to prayer and praise and to fervent gratitude for Your temporal, as well as spiritual, mercies. Help us to remember Your redeeming love; and to renew our exercise of faith in Him who died for our sins and rose again for our justification.

We ask You, O Lord, to send forth Your light to every part of our dark world; and shower down, especially on this nation, the abundance of Your grace, through the diligent and faithful ministry of Your Word among us. Purify every part of Your professing church. Unite us in the bonds of a common faith, and teach us all to love one another.

Give success to every attempt to enlighten the ignorant, to relieve the poor, to comfort the afflicted, to deliver the oppressed from the oppressor, and to promote peace and good will among men. Pour into the hearts of all who know Your truth a spirit of enlarged charity, and raise up many who shall go forth in Your strength, both to multiply their deeds of goodness, and to carry Your gospel into all lands.

We offer these our humble and earnest supplications in the name of Jesus Christ, our blessed and only Savior. Amen.

OUR FATHER in heaven, hallowed be Your name. Your kingdom come. Your will be done on earth as it is in heaven. Give us this day our daily bread. And forgive us our debts, as we forgive our debtors. And do not lead us into temptation, but deliver us from the evil one. For Yours is the kingdom, and the power, and the glory, forever. Amen.

MEMORY VERSE

"You do not know what will happen tomorrow. For what is your life? It is a vapor that appears for a little time, and then vanishes away" (James 4:14).

EVENING PRAYER

GOD, who has appointed a day in which You will judge the world in righteousness, give us grace to test and judge ourselves, that we may not be finally and everlastingly condemned at the judgment seat of Jesus Christ. Dispose us daily to examine both our hearts and lives, for You, O Lord, regard our secret thoughts. Grant to us repentance for whatever sins we have committed, either in thought, word, or deed; and forgive all our trespasses, both against You and against our neighbor, for the sake of Jesus Christ.

We confess that we too easily forget the prize of our high calling in Christ Jesus. You have sent Your Son from heaven to save us. You have set before us an inheritance incorruptible and undefiled, and that fades not away, and You have warned us of a worm that never dies, and of a fire that is not quenched. We beseech You to deliver us from all hardness of heart. May Your Holy

Spirit impress our minds with a deep sense of the importance of eternal things.

May we labor to make our calling and election sure. May we be diligent and hope to the end, knowing that we must soon put off these mortal bodies and that the coming of our Lord Jesus Christ is at hand.

We desire to thank You for the joy of corporate worship and the advantage of a day of rest, for the gift of Your sacred Word, and for all the means of grace. We have abundant light and knowledge; we have line upon line and precept upon precept.

Assist us, this night, to look up to You with pure and humble minds. Let us commit ourselves to Your gracious care, aware of Your constant presence with us. May we desire earnestly to partake both of Your favor here and of those joys that are at Your right hand forevermore. And let not the cares and anxieties of life, nor the legitimate business in which we have been engaged, prevent our now meditating on a better world.

We ask You to grant Your blessing on our dear friends and relations, on our country, and on all for whom we are called to pray. Pity those who are afflicted and who shall pass this night in restlessness and pain. Help the tempted. Give peace to the troubled in mind. Be a Father to the fatherless, and a God of consolation to those who are desolate and oppressed. And give us all grace, that we may have much charity toward one another. Do good to all men, according to our Lord's example and commandment.

Pardon the imperfection of our humble supplications, and grant to us whatsoever things You know to be needful by us, for the sake of Jesus Christ our Savior. Amen.

THE grace of the Lord Jesus Christ, and the love of God, and the communion of the Holy Spirit be with you all. Amen.

MORNING PRAYER

 LMIGHTY LORD OUR GOD, creator of all things, judge of all men, and the merciful Father of all your creatures, we adore You for Your great goodness in providing not only for our temporal necessities but also for the spiritual wants of our souls.

We thank You for Your holy Word, by which we are instructed in Your will and are made aware of our salvation. We thank You for all the means of grace that You have appointed for our edification. We ask You to call our thoughts away, from the fares and activities of this present life, to the consideration of those things that are eternal.

Grant, O Lord, we ask You, that we may not neglect those great religious advantages that we possess in America. May we on Sunday attend reverently to the truths that we can hear and worship You with truly humble and contrite hearts. Prepare our minds to receive the seed, and do not allow us to give way to wandering thoughts, and to an apathetic and worldly spirit. On Sunday may we remember that we are in the house of God, in whose service we are engaged; and it is Your Word that we hear.

And on those days when Your gospel is preached and whenever we read your Word, may we be so awed by the terrors of the Lord, and so affected by the sense of Your mercy, that we may take to heart those truths, so that none of us may receive this grace of God in vain. And when we return from Your house, dispose us all to consider our ways. Let us turn our thoughts to whatever has been improper within us during the past week, let us implore Your mercy in our secret prayers, and let us read with care Your holy Scriptures.

O Lord, help us to consider how few are our days on earth, and how soon we may be called to give an account of the privileges which we have enjoyed, and of the talents committed to us. We have only a short and uncertain life between us and eternal happiness or misery. Let us now redeem the time, before the day of our death shall come and our sentence be sealed everlastingly. Let us make haste to obey Your voice. Let us be diligent in attempting to know Your will; and to understand the doctrines of Your gospel.

And to this end may Your Spirit enlighten and direct us. Guide us into all truth, save us from all ignorance, blindness, and hardness of heart, and preserve us from those delusions that are fatal to the soul. Let us not speak peace to ourselves, when there is no peace; nor hope that we have an interest in Christ, when we have not repented of our sins and have no true faith in His name. O Lord, produce in us sincere repentance. If we are still living in sin, show us, we ask You, our danger. Make us to understand both our own sinfulness and Your mercy, and lead us to the Lamb of God, who takes away the sins of the world.

Bless, we implore You, the ministers of Your gospel. Give great success in their labors. May they, by the word that they shall deliver, awaken those who are yet dead in their sins. May they convince the wavering, establish the weak, comfort the feebleminded, and raise up those who are fallen.

Hear us, O most merciful Lord, in our humble supplications, for the sake of Jesus Christ, our Savior. Amen.

OUR FATHER in heaven, hallowed be Your name. Your kingdom come. Your will be done on earth as it is in heaven. Give us this day our daily bread. And forgive us our debts, as we forgive our debtors. And do not lead us into temptation, but deliver us from the evil one. For Yours is the kingdom, and the power, and the glory, forever. Amen.

MEMORY VERSE

"From childhood you have known the Holy Scriptures, which are able to make you wise for salvation through faith which is in Christ Jesus" (2 Timothy 3:15).

EVENING PRAYER

LMIGHTY AND EVERLASTING GOD, in whose favor is life, and in whose presence there are joys forever, whom angels and archangels continually adore, we whose foundation is in the dust, whose very natures are unholy, desire, nevertheless, to join with all the heavenly host in praising and magnifying Your holy name. We implore, also, that the light of Your reconciled face may shine upon us and that we may be pardoned and accepted in Your sight.

O God, we praise You, we bless You, we glorify Your name, that You have not left us in our low state but have sent salvation to us. We adore You for Your infinite love and mercy, that You have not spared Your only begotten Son but have freely given Him up for us all; that this Lamb has been slain, and this atoning sacrifice has been made for the sins of the world. We thank you that God is in Christ, reconciling the world unto Himself, not holding our trespasses against us.

O Lord, we are sorry that during the past week we have felt so little love toward You who has done such great things for us. We are sorry that earthly things have carried away our thoughts; and that sin has had such dominion over us. We sorrow that the gospel of our salvation has had so little power to make us humble and thankful, spiritually- and heavenly-minded, patient and meek, and diligent in well-doing.

May our hearts be warmed with love to You. May our prayers and our praises ascend with acceptance to the throne of Your grace. May heavenly things occupy our thoughts, and may the world lessen in our esteem.

O God, we stand with shame and sorrow before You, that, even with all the means of grace, we have so little improved our time and talents, have so little honored You by our lives or advanced in true holiness. Day after day we wish to improve our lives, to repent of all our past sins, and to forsake them now and forever. Yet how soon do our hearts again return to the world, and our temptations again come upon us, and overpower us; for our own utmost strength is weakness.

Therefore to You, the God of all might and mercy, do we now pray for grace to serve You. Your face, O Lord, would we seek. On You do we humbly wait, asking You to deliver us from the power and dominion of our sins, and to make Your strength perfect in our weakness.

Make us, from now on, to be more fervent in prayer, and more conscious of our entire dependence on You, and of our infinite obligations to You. Through the gracious help of Your Holy Spirit may we be established in Your most holy ways and endure all dangers and trials of this mortal life; till finally we shall sit down with Christ in His heavenly kingdom.

We offer up our imperfect prayers, in the name of that blessed Mediator. Amen.

THE grace of the Lord Jesus Christ, and the love of God, and the communion of the Holy Spirit be with you all. Amen.

*Prayers of the
Ten Commandments*

THE FIRST COMMANDMENT

You shall have no other gods before Me.

Exodus 20:3

LORD ALMIGHTY, Three Persons and One God, blessed forever, teach us devoutly to adore Your holy Majesty. Enlighten our understandings, sanctify our affections, strengthen our faith, that we may see You, love You, and trust You, according to Your Word and will. You have made Yourself known unto us at various times and in different manners, by the law, the prophets, and the gospel, as our creator, redeemer, and sanctifier.

Grant us grace, we ask You, to live in the perpetual sense of Your presence, and of our continued obligations to You, and of our entire dependence upon You. Enable us to keep You ever in our knowledge, and do not give us over to a reprobate mind but reveal Yourself to us in such a way, by Your blessed Spirit, that in all our thoughts, and words, and actions we may glorify You our God, and be thankful.

We ought to be thankful. Make us thankful for all Your gifts in providence and in grace, since all are Yours. Above all other blessings grant us, O God, a grateful heart, ever looking up to You in faith and love, and desiring to give to Your glory all the talents of the stewardship that You have committed to us.

Other lords have long had dominion over us, and we have served the world, the flesh, and the devil. Day by day we have sinned against You and have indulged our evil tendencies. We have followed the ways and earned the wages of sin. Grant that times past may be the end of these things and that, from now on and forever, we may flee from them. May we cast down all the idols of our hearts and never again bow down to them, but instead take up our cross and follow You.

And in order that the knowledge of Your will may always be spread throughout the world, bless we ask You, the church worldwide, which You have appointed to be a witness and keeper of Your Holy Word; and, especially, bless that pure branch established in these realms. In order that there may never be a lack of a large supply of persons qualified to promote Your glory in every area of society among us, bless, we ask You, the universities and all other seminaries of religious learning. Bless, also, all those who are laboring, whether as pastors or as missionaries, to extend Your kingdom in distant or in foreign lands. And grant, that, in Your good time, and through the single merits of our Lord and Savior, all who now name His name on earth, and all who shall later believe on Him, may be united in Your blessed presence forever. O Lord, hasten that time, and prepare us for it.

Enable us now and forever to feel the solemn obligation of prayer. Worms of the earth, we approach the Lord Jehovah; creatures, we approach our creator; sinners, we approach our judge. In spite of our lowly position, we are permitted and encouraged to remember that this judge took our nature upon Him; while on earth, He taught and commanded His people always to pray. For our sakes He came, and in our flesh He died for us. May His name be blessed forever. Amen.

THE grace of the Lord Jesus Christ, and the love of God, and the communion of the Holy Spirit be with you all. Amen.

THE SECOND COMMANDMENT

*You shall not make for yourself any
carved image, or any likeness of anything
that is in heaven above, or that is in the
earth beneath, or that is in the water under the earth; you shall not bow down to
them nor serve them. For I, the Lord your
God, am a jealous God.*

Exodus 20:4–5

LORD GOD ALMIGHTY, who has
described Yourself as a jealous God not
willing to give Your honor to another,
teach us to worship You with a pure
and holy heart. Enable us always to remember that You are a Spirit, and that You require
those who worship You to worship You in spirit and in
truth. Enable us always to remember that You are love

and that You seek the affections of the creatures whom You have made.

Grant to us, O Lord, we ask You, such a measure of Your grace that we may never mock You by the mere forms of worship, while our hearts are far from You. Instead, may we live in prayer and carry with us continually a sacred sense of Your presence, and whether we eat, or drink, or whatever we do, may we do all to Your glory.

Enlighten us that we may see the evil of our past ways; and strengthen us that we may cast away every idol of this world. May we hate the activities of sin and forever renounce every evil desire that, contrary to Your command and to our Christian profession, we may up to now have retained and cherished.

And teach us to thank You with our whole hearts for the knowledge of Your will and the precepts and promises of Your gospel. As we see the state of the world around us and consider our own privileges, may we remember that of him to whom much is given shall much be required. You have placed us in the midst of light and knowledge, and have given us continual opportunities for serving You, according to Your holy Word. If then the light which is in us be darkness, how great is that darkness.

Grant, blessed Spirit, that our hearts may be renewed by Your grace, so that we may know our blessings and our duties. May we show our gratitude to You for our own portion by giving to others also, through our example and our influence, the light and the privileges that

You have entrusted to us. Teach us ever to know that while in ourselves we can do nothing. Rather, through Christ who strengthens us, we can do all things.

Enable us, then, to spread in the world, by our life and conversation, and by all the means committed to us, the knowledge of Your truth, O Father. Bless the labors of those who are attempting to enlarge the kingdom of your Son, especially in heathen lands. Bring home to His flock all races, tribes, and sects; and take from them all ignorance, hardness of heart, and contempt of Your Word. Grant that they and we may become one fold, under our Lord Jesus, the One Shepherd.

These blessings for ourselves, and for all whom we are bound to remember in our prayers, we humbly ask, O Father Almighty, in the name of our only mediator, the Lord Jesus Christ. Amen.

THE grace of the Lord Jesus Christ, and the love of God, and the communion of the Holy Spirit be with you all. Amen.

THE THIRD
COMMANDMENT

*You shall not take the name of the Lord
your God in vain, for the Lord will not
hold him guiltless who takes His name in
vain.*

Exodus 20:7

LORD ALMIGHTY, help us to approach You with the deepest reverence. In prayer, in praise, and in thanksgiving, may we sense the solemn obligation of calling upon Your name. Grant that we may not mock You by taking Your name in vain by a cold and formal lip-service; but enable us by Your grace to pray with the spirit and to pray with the understanding. In this way our sacrifice may be accepted, and our supplications may be hallowed before You.

And while we dread, unless we should unworthily, and carelessly, and hypocritically draw near to You in prayer, teach us also with watchfulness and concern to avoid every approach to levity and carnality in our daily activities. May we as a habit cultivate truth and purity and sobermindedness in our conversation. Enable us to guard our hearts diligently, and thus to keep our tongues from lying and slandering, from irreverent talking, from foolish jesting, and from blasphemy. And if, in Your good providence, the temptations of some of these sins should not assault us so much or so frequently, as they assault other people, may we labor, more and more, to show forth, through our meekness and charity a holiness that promotes our Christian profession.

You require us to honor You in our hearts and lives, and You have graciously promised that those who honor You, You will honor. Enlighten us by Your grace, we ask You; and teach us hourly to remember that in all our thoughts, conduct, conversations, and actions we are responsible to You. Remind us also that not only for the outward deeds of the body, but for the idle words of our lips, You will call us all to account in the day of judgment. Help us, Lord, in time to repent; and in time to flee from Your wrath to Your mercy, for who can abide Your coming, or stand before Your appearing?

We desire now to confess with meek contrition our past transgressions. We acknowledge with deep humility our present weakness and acknowledge that our only hope and our only strength are in You.

We ask You always to guide and govern our hearts by Your blessed Spirit, and thus to enable us to regulate our tempers, and to purify our minds, and to bridle our tongues. Thus in thought and word as well as in deed we may be gentle and watchful, holy and harmless before You, doing all to Your Glory, O Father Almighty, in the name of the Lord Jesus. We understand that without Him we can do nothing; and that, when we have done all, we are unprofitable servants. Our refuge and salvation are in Him alone.

For His sake, O Lord, and by His words, hear our prayer. Amen.

THE grace of the Lord Jesus Christ, and the love of God, and the communion of the Holy Spirit be with you all. Amen.

THE FOURTH COMMANDMENT

Remember the Sabbath day, to keep it holy.
Exodus 20:8

LORD ALMIGHTY, who as on the sabbath did rest from Your labors and did command us to keep one day in seven holy in remembrance forever, give us grace without doubting to hallow the Lord's Day always before You. May we acknowledge the wisdom and the mercy of this commandment.

Teach us to devote the day, not grudgingly or only of necessity to Your service, but cheerfully and happily. Enable us by Your Holy Spirit to feel that, while this day is a blessing to our wearied bodies, it is also a privilege to our immortal souls. May we be seeking the opportunities of instruction that it gives to ourselves, and be considerate of the opportunities of rest, also, that it may afford to others.

And may we feel, not only that the day is separate as a day of rest from common purposes, but that it is set apart as a day of prayer and praise, of meditation and contrition, of public, social, and secret devotion—for all Your church in all countries.

Teach us, then, Lord, to abstain from all conformity to the levity with which the duties and the privileges of the day are often profaned. May it be our delight to serve You in Your house of prayer; and to withdraw for a while from the world, so that we may be taught and reminded that this world is not our home; that here we have no resting place; that we are strangers and pilgrims, who have professed to seek a heavenly inheritance, a city whose builder and maker is God.

O blessed Jesus, grant us to be in the Spirit on the Lord's Day. May our supplications and our confessions, our prayers and our praises, unite with those of Your faithful people in all nations and languages as the day returns; on that day may the frame of our minds be always more and more conformed to Your will. In so doing, we know we shall be growing into the image of our Lord, and feeling an increasing delight in Your service, and throwing off the chains of sin, and of Satan. In this way may we rise to the full liberty of the children of God; and be fitted, sabbath after sabbath, as we advance in age, for the enjoyment of an eternal sabbath in Your presence in heaven.

To this end, grant that we may have, day by day, a reverent sense of Your presence on earth, and may feel a growing comfort in the thought that You are always near to us. Thus may every day be Your day; and our whole souls and bodies be Yours forever, through Jesus Christ our Lord. Amen.

THE grace of the Lord Jesus Christ, and the love of God, and the communion of the Holy Spirit be with you all. Amen.

THE FIFTH COMMANDMENT

*Honor your father and your mother, that
your days may be long.*

Exodus 20:12

LORD ALMIGHTY, teach us to reverence You above all things, as our Father who is in heaven; and, in obedience to Your will, to carry out all the duties that You have required of us toward the earthly superiors, relations, and friends, with whom Your providence has surrounded us.

Enlighten our understanding that we may realize, and sanctify our hearts that we may feel that our duty is ever our interest. May we know that, while all Your commandments are profitable to those who obey them, You have, in Your infinite mercy, been pleased to give a special honor to Your first commandment with a promise.

Thus you have directed us to look to the earthly blessings that follow obedience, as well as to the glorious reward that You have prepared for Your people in the world to come. But while we freely trust You, and fully desire to obey You, and look forward with humble confidence to the rewards of obedience, enable us, likewise, to recognize that the will to serve You, the power to serve You, and the reward of serving You are all Your gifts alike, and that we can do nothing good without You.

Thus make us to honor our parents still living, showing respect and seeking their counsel. We ask You to make us watchful and diligent in the fulfillment of every relative duty: to all our personal and family connections, to our rulers and to all courts of law, and to all our spiritual pastors. Grant that we may always honor and obey all who are placed over us by Your good providence, and may we pray for them continually. Guard them, O King of Kings, from all dangers, temporal and spiritual; enlighten them, that they may seek, first, their own salvation, and then the good of Your people committed to them. Give wisdom to our counselors and grant them grace to use their influence to the promotion of Your glory in the good of Your church.

Bless all the bishops and pastors of Your flock, and give to us the willing ear and the cheerful heart, so that in teachableness and obedience we may maintain the unity of the spirit in the bond of peace. May we serve

You humbly and in a holy manner in the universal church, of which we are members.

Grant us grace, also, to discharge faithfully and affectionately all our duties in social and domestic life, according to the various tasks to which we may, each of us, have been called. We desire to fulfill all those duties as in Your sight, fearing You and obeying You in love.

These and all things needful for our bodies and our souls, for our temporal and our eternal interests, we ask in the name of Jesus Christ. Amen.

THE grace of the Lord Jesus Christ, and the love of God, and the communion of the Holy Spirit be with you all. Amen.

THE SIXTH COMMANDMENT

You shall not murder.
Exodus 20:13

LORD who has taught us that he who hates his brother without a cause is a murderer, that no murderer has eternal life abiding in him, and that love is the fulfilling of the law, enable us, by Your grace, to govern our hearts and regulate our tempers according to the perfect rule of love. May we ever feel that the indulgence of evil in small things is the most fatal snare of Satan, that an unrestrained look may lead to adultery; and an unrestrained emotion of anger may lead to murder.

May Your blessed Spirit, then, rescue us from the beginnings of sin; and pour into our minds such love for You—and such love, for Your sake, to all our fellow creatures—that no place may be found in us for those temptations of malice and uncharitableness, from which the last guilty deed of murder may proceed. Make us meek and gentle and kind and forgiving. In honor may we prefer one another, not seeking our own, not easily provoked, thinking no evil. May we follow the Spirit of our blessed master, who, when he was reviled, did not revile back but went about doing good; and who taught us, after His example, to love our enemies, to bless them that persecute us, and to overcome evil with good. Whenever the pride and selfishness of our own sinful nature shall resent these lessons, and shall rouse us to wrath and malice, subdue by the working of Your power that rising of anger, which, if indulged, might make us murderers before You, at least in heart.

May we ever remember how much we ourselves sin in all we do, and how much, therefore, we have to be forgiven by You. If, then, You should judge, O Lord, who shall stand?

We have much, indeed, to be forgiven by our neighbor, also. Grant us grace meekly to acknowledge our offenses: our sins before You, and our faults toward our fellow creatures. And while we ask forgiveness for ourselves, may we cheerfully forgive others. And may we labor to do good to them, only working no ill to our neighbors, seeking their welfare, and continually carrying about with us a spirit of compassion ready to relieve the wants of others. We desire a spirit of love ready to forgive their wrongdoing; even as we ourselves hope to be forgiven.

And may the fearful thought recur to our consciences that we may be guilty of endangering our souls, whether by our example in evil, our influence toward evil, by our neglect of doing the good that our duty toward our neighbor required us to do. From such a doom, good Lord, deliver us, and lay not to our charge the sins of those whose souls we may thus have offended. Have mercy upon us, O God, and blot out from the book of Your remembrance all our offenses, all our ignorances, and all our sins. May the grace of Your Holy Spirit watch over us for good, and teach us, in the brotherhood of Christ, to love all Your creatures for His sake. Amen.

*T*HE grace of the Lord Jesus Christ, and the love of God, and the communion of the Holy Spirit be with you all. Amen.

THE SEVENTH COMMANDMENT

You shall not commit adultery.
Exodus 20:14

LORD GOD ALMIGHTY, who has taught us that without holiness no man shall see You, and has commanded us to be holy as You are holy, enable us now and forever to overcome all corrupt affections. May we serve You in body, soul, and spirit, being renewed and sanctified by Your grace.

Enable us ever to remember that we carry about an evil heart and a frail and feeble nature, that we are daily battered with infirmities, and that we have to struggle with temptations from within and from without. Teach us, therefore, to make a covenant with our eyes that they do not look on anything which may lead us to evil. Teach us to make a covenant with our imaginations that they abstain from all approaches to sin. And teach us habitually to feel and fear our own weakness, and to tremble, unless, by yielding to the least indulgence in unlawful things, we should grieve Your blessed Spirit, and, finally losing the power of resistance, we should be drawn into everlasting destruction.

Blessed Jesus, save us from this awful state. You, O God, see us now. You see us always. You know whether we are deceiving ourselves, and mocking You; or whether we really and solemnly desire to be saved from the power of Satan and to be made forever holy and happy beings before You. Grant that we may never speak peace to ourselves, when there is no peace; or indulge the false hope that we have attained the purity that You require by abstaining, if we have abstained, from the grosser sins of the flesh.

Enlighten us to see that You command us to be pure in heart if we hope to see You. Convince us, by Your Holy Spirit, that the pleasures of sin are but for a time, and that, even in this world, those pleasures lead to death, or are fleeting, and unworthy of immortal natures.

O Father of purity, enable us to feel, that even a look may be sin; and that unrepented sin is death. Grant us grace, then, to avoid every thought, word, and action that is displeasing to Your holy nature, and to crucify the flesh with its desires and lusts. Enable us to control our bodies, and to bring them into subjection; and to abstain from all appearance of evil; and may our hearts be a suitable habitation for Your blessed Spirit, this day and forever.

Blessed Spirit, enter, then, into those hearts; and evermore dwell in them. Guard us and all Your people, and all for whom we are bound to pray, from every spiritual and every fleshly wickedness, and make us Yours now and forever, for the sake of Jesus Christ. Amen.

THE grace of the Lord Jesus Christ, and the love of God, and the communion of the Holy Spirit be with you all. Amen.

THE EIGHTH COMMANDMENT

You shall not steal.
Exodus 20:15

LORD GOD, from whom alone proceed all the good things that we enjoy, who has determined the limits of our dwelling, and has allotted to each of us such a share of Your gifts as You see best for us, grant us the further and greater blessing: to receive our portion at Your hands not only with contentment, but with gratitude.

We are unworthy, O Lord, of the least of all Your mercies. Enable us to employ them heartily in Your service and to do good in our generation with the talents that You have entrusted to us. Grant that we may be ever watchful and ever active, continually aware of the unseen realities of heaven and hell. May we mortify all the corrupt affections of earth, not seeking the wealth of this world as a good but receiving it, if, in the course of Your providence, it shall be committed to us, reverently as a trust. Whether it be much or little, may we be grateful with what we have.

Enlighten our understandings and sanctify our desires, so that we may never seek that which You have forbidden, or injure our neighbor in respect to that which You have bestowed upon him. May we be guarded from the inordinate selfishness that our fallen nature too often exhibits, and may we do unto all men whatever we would that they should do unto us.

And lest we should yield to great sins, enable us, God, to avoid the least sins, and to guard against every approach to evil. Grant us grace not only to keep our hands from picking and stealing, but to keep our hearts, also, from every inordinate desire. Pour down upon us, we ask You, your Holy Spirit, that we may never deceive ourselves or direct ourselves in any false way, such as speaking peace to ourselves when there is no peace or wronging our neighbor by the indulgence of any covetous desire or any selfish and greedy act. Grant us grace to render to all their dues: tribute to whom tribute is due, custom to whom custom. And give us tender consciences, O God, that we may not defraud our brother in any matter, but may always act toward him and toward You as those who are hereafter to give account before Your awful throne.

Make us ever mindful that the time is coming when the gold and silver of this world will be corroded; and when at last, if not even now, we shall see the folly and the guilt of heaping up ungodly treasure together for the last days. We brought nothing into the world, and we shall carry nothing out of it; the only question then will be whether we have been faithful in the stewardship that Your good providence may have entrusted us.

Enable us, O Lord, to see that only Your grace can make us faithful in this way; and enable us also always to feel that, whatever else You may grant, or withhold, You will always give the Holy Spirit to them who ask it. Empower us then with Your Holy Ghost, for the sake of our only mediator and advocate, Jesus Christ. Amen.

THE grace of the Lord Jesus Christ, and the love of God, and the communion of the Holy Spirit be with you all. Amen.

THE NINTH COMMANDMENT

You shall not bear false witness against your neighbor.

Exodus 20:16

GOD, who has taught us that all our doings without love are worth nothing, and that love is the fulfilling of the law, pour out into our hearts Your blessed Spirit, that we may daily be renewed in the exercises of every Christian grace toward You and toward our neighbor. Teach us to love You above all things, and to love our neighbor as ourselves.

As the God of all truth and holiness, strengthen us that we may flee from every snare of the devil, who is the father of lies. Enlighten and direct us, that we may always speak truth to our neighbor, and that, while we avoid all malice and deceit toward him, we may likewise avoid all hypocrisy toward You.

Shed the Spirit of wisdom from above into our souls, that we may be pure and peaceable, gentle and docile, full of mercy and good fruits. We are taught by Your holy apostle James that the tongue no one can tame if he trust to his own strength or wisdom; thus enable us, O God, to bridle it and the whole body. Grant us grace that we may not think it enough to avoid falsehood when we call upon You solemnly to listen to us; but may we constantly guard against all those temptations and actions that may lead us in smaller things to violate truth. Keep us from being inconsiderate, lazy, and vain, which may cause us to injure our fellow creatures for our own pleasure. Guard us from the deeper sins of malice and envy, which may allow us to injure another person by deliberate falsehood.

In all our thoughts may we have You, blessed Jesus, ever before us; and in all our communications with the world around us, may we desire to act as in Your presence. While we deal charitably and truly with our neighbor, may we still be strengthened by a holy boldness in Your sight—not ashamed of You and of Your Word, when the cause of truth shall require us to speak out, but ever ready to maintain right against wrong. And may we be willing to contend earnestly for the faith and, when You shall require us, to go forth in Your name against all gainsayers. Yet teach us ever, in Your own Spirit, to prefer a lowly and charitable conversation with all men, at all times speaking the truth in love. And whenever Your honor shall require it, may we speak that truth, if it be against our neighbor, simply because Your honor does require it.

Finally, grant us grace ever to bless You with our tongues; and, still more, in our hearts and lives, as well as with our lips, to show forth Your praise.

THE grace of the Lord Jesus Christ, and the love of God, and the communion of the Holy Spirit be with you all. Amen.

THE TENTH
COMMANDMENT

You shall not covet your neighbor's house;
you shall not covet your neighbor's wife
. . . nor anything that is your neighbor's.

Exodus 20:17

LMIGHTY GOD, to whom all hearts are open, and from whom no secret desire can be concealed, grant us, we ask You, such a measure of Your blessed Spirit, that we may both discern Your will and faithfully perform it.

You have commanded us in Your Word not merely to abstain from gross sins, from adultery, and from theft, but to avoid every thought and wish of evil, and every covetous inclination. Grant us grace to always remember that You require piety and self-denial and holiness in the inner man; and not only the outward service of our

words and bodies, but the absence of every sinful imagination. Enable us, then, we implore You, to cut off the
right hand, and to pluck out the right eye that may
cause us to offend; and teach us to restrain every type of
sin in our souls.

Enable us, in respect to the things of this world, to be
contented and thankful; in prosperity, to be meek and
humble; in adversity, to be resigned and cheerful; and,
in every trial of life, to seek not our own will, but Your
will alone.

Teach us, day by day, to guard more and more the
state of our heart, for out of it come the issues of life.
How easily may we deceive our neighbors by our outward conduct and profession. How fatally we may deceive ourselves, but You are not deceived; and in all our
evil thoughts, in all our covetous desires, in all our sinful
imaginations, which we have indulged, Your eye has
been upon us. May the awful truth be from now on always present in our souls. You, God, see us. You have
known all the secret transgressions of the heart; and You
will now bring our desires, as well as our works, into
judgment, unless they are repented of, forsaken, and
blotted out by the blood of Jesus.

Pardon, God, for Christ's sake, all in our past lives
that has been displeasing to You; strengthen us in the
days which may yet be to come; and grant us wisdom
and grace to abstain from every thought of evil.

And while we confess our past offenses, and feel and
deplore our present weakness, and acknowledge that our

only help and our only strength are in You, teach us to thank You with our whole hearts for Your longsuffering providence. For in the midst of all our transgressions, You have surrounded us with so many mercies of this life, especially with the means of grace and with the hope of glory.

Grant, Almighty God, that we may display forth our sense of Your goodness by dedicating ourselves anew to Your service. Enable us to take up our cross and to follow You, to abstain from every sin and to flee from every snare. Help us to regulate every desire of our minds, and to let our light so shine forth in our lives that others, seeing our good works, may, with us, glorify You, through whose grace alone those good works proceed.

We ask every blessing in the name of Jesus Christ; and in His words desire to conclude our prayers. Amen.

THE grace of the Lord Jesus Christ, and the love of God, and the communion of the Holy Spirit be with you all. Amen.